The Wadsworth Themes in American Literature Series

1910–1945

THEME 15

Racism and Activism

Martha J. Cutter
University of Connecticut

Jay Parini
Middlebury College
General Editor

Australia • Brazil • Japan • Korea • Mexico • Singapore • Spain • United Kingdom • United States

WADSWORTH
CENGAGE Learning™

The Wadsworth Themes in American Literature Series, 1910–1945
Theme 15 Racism and Activism
Martha J. Cutter, Jay Parini

Publisher, Humanities: *Michael Rosenberg*

Senior Development Editor: *Michell Phifer*

Assistant Editor: *Megan Garvey*

Editorial Assistant: *Rebekah Matthews*

Associate Development Project Manager: *Emily A. Ryan*

Executive Marketing Manager: *Mandee Eckersley*

Senior Marketing Communications Manager: *Stacey Purviance*

Senior Project Manager, Editorial Production: *Lianne Ames*

Senior Art Director: *Cate Rickard Barr*

Senior Print Buyer: *Mary Beth Hennebury*

Permissions Editor: *Margaret Chamberlain-Gaston*

Permissions Researcher: *Writers Research Group, LLC*

Production Service: *Kathy Smith*

Text Designer: *Frances Baca*

Photo Manager: *Sheri Blaney*

Photo Researcher: *Lili Weiner*

Cover Designer: *Frances Baca*

Cover Image: © *Photograph by Charles Peterson*

Compositor: *Graphic World, Inc.*

Library of Congress Control Number: 2008925323

ISBN-13: 978-1-4282-6258-4

ISBN-10: 1-4282-6258-X

Wadsworth Cengage Learning
25 Thomson Place
Boston, 02210
USA

Cengage Learning products are represented in Canada by Nelson Education, Ltd.

For your course and learning solutions, visit **academic.cengage.com.**

Purchase any of our products at your local college store or at our preferred online store **www.ichapters.com.**

The credits on page 94 constitute an extension of the copyright page.

Printed in the United States of America
1 2 3 4 5 6 7 12 11 10 09 08

Contents

Preface

WHAT IS AMERICA? HOW HAVE WE DEFINED OURSELVES over the past five centuries, and dealt with the conflict of cultures, the clash of nations, races, ethnicities, religious visions, and class interests? How have we thought about ourselves, as men and women, in terms of class and gender? How have we managed to process a range of complex and compelling issues?

The Wadsworth Themes in American Literature Series addresses these questions in a sequence of 21 booklets designed especially for classroom use in a broad range of courses. There is nothing else like them on the market. Each booklet has been carefully edited to frame issues of importance, with attention to the development of key themes. Teachers and students have consistently found these mini-anthologies immensely productive in the classroom, as the texts we have chosen are provocative, interesting to read, and central to the era under discussion. Each thematic booklet begins with a short essay that provides the necessary historical and literary context to address the issues raised in that theme. In addition, many of the headnotes have been written by scholars, with an eye to introducing students to the life and times of the author under discussion, paying attention to historical context as well, and making sure to prepare the way for the selection that follows. The footnotes provide useful glosses on words and phrases, keying the reader to certain historical moments or ideas, explaining oddities, offering extra material to make the texts more accessible.

Each of these themes is drawn from *The Wadsworth Anthology of American Literature,* which is scheduled for later publication. The first sequence of booklets, edited by Ralph Bauer at the University of Maryland, takes in the colonial period, which runs from the arrival of Columbus in the New World through 1820, a period of immense fluidity and dynamic cultural exchange. Bauer is a pioneering scholar who takes a hemispheric approach to the era, looking at the crush of cultures—Spanish, English, Dutch, German, French; each of these European powers sent colonial missions across the Atlantic Ocean, and the collision of these cultures with each other and with the Native American population (itself diverse and complicated) was combustive. Bauer isolates several themes, one of which is called "Between Cultures," and looks at the confrontation of European and Native American traditions. In "Spirituality, Church, and State in Colonial America," he examines the obsession with religious ideas, some of which led to the crisis in Salem, where the infamous witch trials occurred. In "Empire,

Science, and the Economy in the Americas," the focus shifts to the material basis for culture, and how it affected some outlying regions, such as Barbados, Peru, Mexico, and Alaska—thus blasting apart the rigid ways that scholars have more traditionally thought about North America in isolation. In "Contested Nations in the Early Americas," Bauer centers on revolutionary fervor in places like Haiti, Cuba, and Jamaica, where various groups fought for control of both territory and cultural influence.

In the second sequence of booklets, Shirley Samuels (who is Professor of English and American Studies at Cornell and has established herself as a major voice in the field of nineteenth-century American literature) looks at the early days of the American republic, a period stretching from 1800 to 1865, taking us through the Civil War. This was, of course, a period of huge expansion as well as consolidation. Manifest Destiny was a catchword, as the original thirteen colonies expanded in what Robert Frost referred to as "a nation gradually realizing westward." The question of identity arose on different fronts, and we see the beginnings of the women's movement here. In her first theme, Samuels looks at "The Woman Question," offering a selection of texts by men and women thinking about the place of a woman in society and in the home. Some of this writing is quite provocative, and much of it is rarely studied in college classrooms.

The racial questions came into focus during this era, too, and the groundwork for the Civil War was unhappily laid. In "Confronting Race," Samuels offers a searing medley of texts from Black Hawk through Frances E. W. Harper. These works hurl this topic into stark relief against a cultural landscape in perpetual ferment. This booklet includes selections from the speeches of Sojourner Truth, the pseudonym of an astonishing black woman, a former slave who became a leading abolitionist and advocate for women's rights.

In "Manifest Destiny and the Quest for the West," Samuels offers a mix of classic and lesser known texts on the theme of westward expansion, beginning with the remarkable *Journals of Lewis and Clark*, a key document in the literature of westward expansion and a vivid example of the literature of exploration. She ends with "Views of War," presenting a range of inspiring and heart-rending texts from a time of bloodshed, hatred, and immense idealism. The Union was very nearly broken, and one gets a full sense of the dynamics of this troubled era by comparing these texts by an unusual range of authors from Oliver Wendell Holmes and Julia Ward Howe through Sidney Lanier, one of the finest (if lesser known) poets of the era.

In the third sequence of booklets, Alfred Bendixen, who teaches at Texas A&M University, offers a selection from the period just after the Civil War through the beginnings of the modern period. Bendixen, who presides over the American Literature Association, has proven himself a scholar of unusual talents, and he brings his deep knowledge of the period into play here. In "Imagining Gender," he takes up where Samuels left off, looking at a compelling range of texts by men and women who consider the evolving issue of gender in fascinating ways. One sees the coalescing of the women's movement in some of this work, and also the resistance that inevitably arose, as women tried to assert themselves and to find their voice.

In "Questions of Social and Economic Justice," Bendixen puts forward texts by a range of key figures, including George Washington Cable, Hamlin Garland, Mary Wilkins Freeman, and Jack London. Each of these gifted writers meditates on the struggle of a young nation to define itself, to locate its economic pulse, to balance the need for economic expansion and development with the requirements and demands of social justice. Many of these themes carry forward into the twentieth century, and it is worth looking closely at the origins of these themes in an era of compulsive growth. Needless to say, this was also a period when millions of immigrants arrived from Southern and Eastern Europe, radically changing the complexion of the nation. Bendixen offers a unique blend of texts on the conflicts and questions that naturally followed the so-called Great Migration in "Immigration, Ethnicity, and Race." This section includes excerpts from Jane Addams's remarkable memoir of her time at Hull-House, a mansion in Chicago where she and her coworkers offered a range of social assistance and cultural programs to working class immigrants.

The most unusual theme in this sequence of booklets by Bendixen is "Crime, Mystery, and Detection." Here the student will find an array of gripping stories by some of the original authors in a field that forms the basis for contemporary popular fiction around the world. American readers in this period loved detective stories, and readers still do. The mix is quite unusual, and it remains fascinating to see how the genre found its legs and began to run, through a time when readers wished to apply all the tools of intelligence to their world, discovering its ways and meaning, trying to figure out "who done it" in so many ways.

Martha J. Cutter—a scholar of considerable range and achievement who now teaches at the University of Connecticut—edits the sequence of booklets dealing with the modern era, 1910–1945, a period of huge importance in American history and culture. The American empire came into its own in this era, recognized its muscles, and began to flex them—in ways productive and (at times) destructive. Cutter begins by looking at the women's movement, and how men reacted to certain inevitable pressures. In "The Making of the New Woman and the New Man," she charts the struggle between the sexes in a compelling range of texts, including works by Sui Sin Far, Edwin Arlington Robinson, James Weldon Johnson, Willa Cather, and John Steinbeck, among others. Of course, the subject of class had a massive impact on how people viewed themselves, and in "Modernism and the Literary Left," she presents a selection of works that deal with issues of class, money, and power. At the center of this sequence lies "May Day," one of F. Scott Fitzgerald's most luminous and provocative stories.

The New Negro Renaissance occurred during this period, a revival and consolidation of writing in a variety of genres by African Americans. Here Cutter offers a brilliant selection of key texts from this movement, including work by Langston Hughes and Zora Neale Hurston in "Racism and Activism." This booklet extends well beyond the Harlem Renaissance itself to work by Richard Wright, a major voice in African American literature.

As it must, the theme of war occupies a central place in one thematic booklet. In the first half of the twentieth century, world wars destroyed the lives of millions. Never had the world seen killing like this, or inhumanity and cruelty on a scale that beggars the imagination. The violence of these conflicts, and the cultural implications of such destruction, necessarily held the attention of major writers. And so, in "Poetry and Fiction of War and Social Conflict," we find a range of compelling work by such writers as Ezra Pound, H.D. (Hilda Doolittle), T. S. Eliot, and Edna St. Vincent Millay.

Henry Hart is a contemporary poet, biographer, and critic with a broad range of work to his credit (he holds a chair in literature at William and Mary College). His themes are drawn from the postwar era, and he puts before readers a seductive range of work by poets, fiction writers, and essayists. Many of the themes from earlier volumes continue here. For instance, Hart begins with "Race and Ethnicity in the Melting Pot," offering students a chance to think hard about the matter of ethnicity and race in contemporary America. With texts by James Baldwin and Malcolm X through Amy Tan and Ana Menéndez, he presents viewpoints that will prove challenging and provocative—perfect vehicles for classroom discussion.

In "Class Conflicts and the American Dream," Hart explores unstable, challenging terrain in a sequence of texts by major postwar authors from Martin Luther King, Jr. through Flannery O'Connor. Some of these works are extremely well known, such as John Updike's story, "A & P." Others, such as James Merrill's "The Broken Home" may be less familiar. This booklet, as a whole, provides a rich field of texts, and will stimulate discussion on many levels about the role of class in American society.

Similarly, Hart puts forward texts that deal with gender and sexuality in "Exploring Gender and Sexual Norms." From Sylvia Plath's wildly destructive poem about her father, "Daddy," through the anguished meditations in poetry of Adrienne Rich, Anne Sexton, Allen Ginsberg, and Frank O'Hara (among others), the complexities of sexuality and relationships emerge. In Gore Vidal's witty and ferocious look at homosexuality and anti-Semitism in "Pink Triangle and Yellow Star," students have an opportunity to think hard about things that are rarely put forward in frank terms. Further meditations on masculinity and as well as gay and lesbian sexualities occur in work by Pat Califia, Robert Bly, and Mark Doty. The section called "Witnessing War" offers some remarkable poems and stories by such writers as Robert Lowell, James Dickey, and Tim O'Brien—each of them writing from a powerful personal experience. In a medley of texts on "Religion and Spirituality," Hart explores connections to the sacred, drawing on work by such writers as Flannery O'Connor, Charles Wright, and Annie Dillard. As in earlier booklets, these thematic arrangements by Hart will challenge, entertain, and instruct.

In sum, we believe these booklets will stimulate conversations in class that should be productive as well as memorable, for teacher and student alike. The texts have been chosen because of their inherent interest and readability, and—in a sense—for the multiple ways in which they "talk" to each other. Culture is, of course, nothing more than good conversation, its elevation to a level of discourse. We, the editors of these thematic booklets, believe that the attractive arrangements of compelling texts will make a lasting impression, and will help to answer the question posed at the outset: What is America?

ACKNOWLEDGMENTS

We would like to thank the following readers and scholars who helped us shape this series: Brian Adler, Valdosta State University; John Alberti, Northern Kentucky University; Lee Alexander, College of William and Mary; Althea Allard, Community College of Rhode Island; Jonathan Barron, University of Southern Mississippi; Laura Behling, Gustavus Adolphus College; Peter Bellis, University of Alabama at Birmingham; Alan Belsches, Troy University Dothan Campus; Renee Bergland, Simmons College; Roy Bird, University of Alaska Fairbanks; Michael Borgstrom, San Diego State University; Patricia Bostian, Central Peidmont Community College; Jessica Bozek, Boston University; Lenore Brady, Arizona State University; Maria Brandt, Monroe Community College; Martin Buinicki, Valparaiso University; Stuart Burrows, Brown University; Shawrence Campbell, Stetson University; Steven Canaday, Anne Arundel Community College; Carole Chapman, Ivy Tech Community College of Indiana; Cheng Lok Chua, California State University; Philip Clark, McLean High School; Matt Cohen, Duke University; Patrick Collins, Austin Community College; Paul Cook, Arizona State University; Dean Cooledge, University of Maryland Eastern Shore; Howard Cox, Angelina College; Laura Cruse, Northwest Iowa Community College; Ed Dauterich, Kent State University; Janet Dean, Bryant University; Rebecca Devers, University of Connecticut; Joseph Dewey, University of Pittsburgh–Johnstown; Christopher Diller, Berry College; Elizabeth Donely, Clark College; Stacey Donohue, Central Oregon Community College; Douglas Dowland, The University of Iowa; Jacqueline Doyle, California State University, East Bay; Robert Dunne, Central Connecticut State University; Jim Egan, Brown University; Marcus Embry, University of Northern Colorado; Nikolai Endres, Western Kentucky University; Terry Engebretsen, Idaho State University; Jean Filetti, Christopher Newport University; Gabrielle Foreman, Occidental College; Luisa Forrest, El Centro College; Elizabeth Freeman, University of California–Davis; Stephanie Freuler, Valencia Community College; Andrea Frisch, University of Maryland; Joseph Fruscione, Georgetown University; Lisa Giles, University of Southern Maine; Charles Gongre, Lamar State College–Port Arthur;

Gary Grieve-Carlson, Lebanon Valley College; Judy Harris, Tomball College; Brian Henry, University of Richmond; Allan Hikida, Seattle Central Community College; Lynn Houston, California State University, Chico; Coleman Hutchison, University of Texas–Austin; Andrew Jewell, University of Nebraska–Lincoln; Marion Kane, Lake-Sumter Community College; Laura Knight, Mercer County Community College; Delia Konzett, University of New Hampshire; Jon Little, Alverno College; Chris Lukasik, Purdue University; Martha B. Macdonald, York Technical College; Angie Macri, Pulaski Technical College; John Marsh, University of Illinois at Urbana Champaign; Christopher T. McDermot, University of Alabama; Jim McWilliams, Dickinson State University; Joe Mills, North Carolina School of the Arts; Bryan Moore, Arkansas State University; James Nagel, University of Georgia; Wade Newhouse, Peace College; Keith Newlin, University of North Carolina Wilmington; Andrew Newman, Stony Brook University; Brian Norman, Idaho State University; Scott Orme, Spokane Community College; Chris Phillips, Lafayette College; Jessica Rabin, Anne Arundel Community College; Audrey Raden, Hunter College; Catherine Rainwater, St. Edward's University; Rick Randolph, Kaua; Joan Reeves, Northeast Alabama Community College; Paul Reich, Rollins College; Yelizaveta Renfro, University of Nebraska–Lincoln; Roman Santillan, College of Staten Island; Marc Schuster, Montgomery County Community College; Carol Singley, Rutgers–Camden; Brenda Siragusa, Corinthian Colleges Inc.; John Staunton, University of North Caroline–Charlotte; Ryan Stryffeler, Ivy Tech Community College of Indiana; Robert Sturr, Kent State University, Stark Campus; James Tanner, University of North Texas; Alisa Thomas, Toccoa Falls College; Nathan Tipton, The University of Memphis; Gary Totten, North Dakota State University; Tony Trigilio, Columbia College, Chicago; Pat Tyrer, West Texas A&M University; Becky Villarreal, Austin Community College; Edward Walkiewicz, Oklahoma State University; Jay Watson, University of Mississippi; Karen Weekes, Penn State Abington; Bruce Weiner, St. Lawrence University; Cindy Weinstein, California Institute of Technology; Stephanie Wells, Orange Coast College; Robert West, Mississippi State University; Diane Whitley Bogard, Austin Community College–Eastview Campus; Edlie Wong, Rutgers; and Beth Younger, Drake University.

In addition, we would like to thank the indefatigable staff at Cengage Learning/Wadsworth for their tireless efforts to make these booklets and the upcoming anthology a reality: Michael Rosenberg, Publisher; Michell Phifer, Senior Development Editor, Lianne Ames, Senior Content Project Manager, Megan Garvey, Assistant Editor; Rebekah Matthews, Editorial Assistant, Emily Ryan, Associate Development Project Manager, Mandee Eckersley, Managing Marketing Manager, Stacey Purviance, Marketing Communications Manager, and Cate Barr, Art Director. We would also like to thank Kathy Smith, Project Manager, for her patience and attention to detail.

—Jay Parini, Middlebury College

Racism and Activism

The authors of the Harlem Renaissance believed that they could use their writing to change the dominant culture's view of African Americans. W. E. B. DuBois coined the phrase "all art is propaganda" to reflect his view that an art movement created by African Americans would change the way African Americans were perceived and treated by white society. But as the decades of the 1920s and 1930s passed, it became apparent that whereas art might have attacked the ideology of racism, more concrete political action was needed. Lynching was rampant, segregation in education and the military persisted, and the Ku Klux Klan flourished, reaching its peak membership rate in the 1920s, when the organization included about 15 percent of the nation's eligible population.

It also became clear that African Americans were still disenfranchised in many political and economic systems. And so in the 1930s a new militancy developed, a commitment to direct mechanisms for the achievement of political change.

The new militancy was fueled in part by changing economic conditions; when the stock market collapsed in 1929 and the "roaring twenties" ended, the "vogue" of Harlem also ended. European American patronage of Harlem establishments and artists declined and in general African Americans lost their jobs at faster rates than European Americans, causing foreclosures on mortgages and evictions from rental properties. The despair and anger over these economic conditions led to what has been characterized by sociologist Allen D. Grimshaw as "the first modern race riot," the Harlem Riot of 1935 (a riot in which residents of Harlem destroyed two million dollars' worth of white-owned commercial property). Events that symbolized the institutionalized racism of the nation—such as the infamous trial of the "Scottsboro Boys" (nine black teenagers falsely accused of raping two white women on a train as it passed through Scottsboro, Alabama)—riveted a nation and seemed to indicate that art alone was not enough, that political, social, and economic change must also occur.

Ku Klux Klan membership was on the rise in the 1920s. Klan members march down Pennsylvania Avenue in Washington, D.C. in 1928.
Courtesy National Archives

Many of the writers from this time period moved on from the so-called primitivism of the Harlem Renaissance to embrace "proletarian literature," writing that

The trial of the "Scottsboro Boys"—nine men falsely accused of raping two white women on a train—attracted national and international attention, sparking debates and near riots.
© Bettmann/CORBIS

focused on class position, in addition to race. Specific reforms were advocated: Richard Wright was involved with Communism, Marcus Garvey proposed that African Americans claim land in Africa, and Walter White advocated the desegregation of the military and schools and promoted (unsuccessfully) an anti-lynching law. There was also a new militancy in the tone and voice of many of these writers. Marcus Garvey, for example, indicates in his "Speech on Disarmament" that African Americans will not be content to sit by and watch as other nations decide their fate: "The new Negro is going to strike back or is going to die. . . . Now the world of oppressed peoples have got the spirit of liberty and from far-off India we hear the cry of a free and independent India; . . . the Negro loves peace; the Negro likes to disarm, but the Negro says to the world, 'Let us have justice; let us have equity; let us have freedom; let us have democracy indeed' . . . until then, I repeat, there will be wars and rumors of wars." Garvey was one of the first to criticize the way Britain had colonized Africa and India and to advocate self-rule for former colonies. Garvey also advocated a "back-to-Africa" movement that would relocate African Americans to a self-governing area of Africa. In his life and actions, Walter White took a similarly militant stand, using his white skin to "pass" for white and investigate lynching and race riots, and insisting on concrete political reforms. White was unsuccessful in establishing anti-lynching laws, but as executive secretary of the NAACP (the National Association for the Advancement of Colored People) for over twenty-five years, he was involved in a number of successful legal actions, such as the landmark 1954 decision *Brown* v. *Board of Education of Topeka*, which overturned the "separate but equal" ruling in education and led (eventually) to the desegregation of many schools.

Writers such as Marita Bonner and Zora Neale Hurston, on the other hand, may appear to be advocating no direct political change in their works. They write instead about the harm that racism does to young, developing psyches. Yet, in "How It Feels to Be

Activists such as Walter White worked tirelessly for the desegregation of schools, not achieved until 1954 when the Supreme Court ruled in *Brown v. Board of Education* that segregation based on race was unconstitutional.
© Bettmann/CORBIS

Colored Me," Hurston's portrayal of how racism affects her young self may become an instrument of social change if it effectively moves individuals to wonder why racism does exist, and if it must continue to exist. Moreover, many of these writers specifically examined (more directly than earlier writers) the link between art and social change. As Kay Boyle indicates in her poem "A Communication to Nancy Cunard," art could be an instrument of social change when combined with more direct interventions (legal, political, and economic) into society. Many of the writers from this time period viewed themselves as both artists and activists.

Some writers of this era believed that art needed to be direct, focused on "the masses," and clear in its ideological agenda. Richard Wright's "The Ethics of Living Jim Crow" is an example of this type of direct art. Wright was involved with the Communist Party literary journal *New Masses,* set up to promote proletarian art. Wright disagreed to some extent with the Communist Party's views and he did not feel that art had to be as straightforward as a political pamphlet. However, its purpose needed to be clear. Furthermore, Wright criticized Zora Neale Hurston's writing, accusing her of burlesquing her race, of making African Americans into stereotypes and caricatures. Hurston responded in a letter that she tried to chart a middle ground: "I tried . . . not to pander to the folks who expect a clown and a villain in every Negro. Neither did I want to pander to those 'race' people among us who see nothing but perfection in all of us."

Treading a middle ground between the concepts of "direct art" advocated by Wright and the more indirect portrayals of the effect of racism on developing psyches found in Bonner and Hurston are works by Jean Toomer, Langston Hughes, and Sterling Brown. In some of these works, lynching becomes a central symbol of the injustices of a white society and the need for black activism; texts such as Toomer's "Blood-Burning Moon" and Hughes's "Song for a Dark Girl" graphically depict such violence, gesturing towards a direct and specific political solution in the anti-lynching laws being advocated by Walter White. In "Remembering Nat Turner" Sterling Brown recounts one response to racism and violence: Nat Turner's bloody revolution of 1831, in which an insurgent band of slaves killed fifty-seven white men, women, and children before their revolt was suppressed. Poems such as this one suggest that militant and armed struggle might be one solution to racist violence, while others such as Brown's "Strong Men" and Hughes's "Mulatto" suggest that endurance and peaceful resistance, rather than violence, might be the most effective political solution.

Art as a form of activism—as something that molds and shapes the racial consciousness of both African Americans and whites—therefore was not forgotten in this time period. However, tensions existed about how art interacted with more concrete forms of action and about what type of art would best function as an instrument of social change.

Marcus Garvey 1887–1940

Today, Marcus Garvey is remembered as an early proponent of the back-to-Africa movement, but he was also an important writer, speaker, publisher, journalist, and entrepreneur. Garvey dreamed of blacks finding a permanent homeland in the country of Liberia in Africa: "Our success educationally, industrially and politically is based upon the protection of a nation founded by ourselves. And the nation can be nowhere else but in Africa."

Garvey's life was turbulent. The youngest of eleven children, he was born in Jamaica and traveled widely in Central America and South America. In 1914, Garvey organized the Universal Negro Improvement Association (UNIA)—an international self-help organization—and in 1920 the organization held its first convention in New York. Speaking before a crowd of more than twenty-five thousand people, Garvey discussed his dream of an African nation. His ideas were lauded and thousands became members of the UNIA; the organization soon had branches in more than forty countries. However, the UNIA eventually began to decline in popularity and Garvey became ensnared in legal problems that eventually led to his imprisonment. In 1927, his sentence was commuted and he was deported to Jamaica by President Calvin Coolidge. Garvey died in England in 1940.

In the speech reprinted here from 1921, Garvey emphasizes that blacks' absence from an important conference on disarmament represents their general absence in the world of politics at large. More importantly, Garvey emphasizes that blacks must take steps to remedy this political absence, they must "arm through organization." He critiques colonization—the dominance of small, impoverished nations by large, wealthy ones—and warns that no peace can be achieved until this dominance ends.

Further Reading Winston James, *Holding Aloft the Banner of Ethiopia: Caribbean Radicalism in Early Twentieth-Century America* (1998); Tony Martin, *African Fundamentalism: A Literary and Cultural Anthology of Garvey's Harlem Renaissance* (1991); Judith Stein, *The World of Marcus Garvey: Race and Class in Modern Society* (1986).

Speech on Disarmament Conference Delivered at Liberty Hall, New York, U.S.A. Nov. 6, 1921

Just at this time the world is again preparing for a reorganization. Since the war of 1914[1] the world became disorganized. Many conferences have been held, in which statesmen of all the reputable governments have taken part, for the purpose of settling a world policy, by which humanity and the world could return to normal. Several of the conferences were held in France, others in Switzerland and England. On

[1] **war of 1914:** World War I.

the 11th of this month will assemble in Washington what is to be known as an Armament Conference. At this conference statesmen from Great Britain and her self-governing dominions, statesmen from France, Japan, China, Norway, Holland and several other countries will there assemble and partake in the discussion for regulating the armaments of the world.

Every race will be represented at that conference except the Negro race. It is a sad confession to make, nevertheless it is true. The world wants to return to normal and the only people preventing it from returning to normal, apparently, are the white and yellow peoples, and they only are taken into account. I suppose after they have met and discussed the issues, the world will return to normal, but I believe someone has a second thought coming. I have no faith in the disarmament plan of the nations. I am a pessimist as far as disarmament goes. I do not believe that man will disarm until there is universal justice. Any attempt at disarming when half of the world oppresses the other half is but a farce, because the oppressed half will make somebody get armed sooner or later, and I hope Negroes will pay no attention to what is said and what is done at the conference. It does not concern you one bit. Disarmament may sound good for heaven and paradise, but not for this world that we live in, where we have so many robbers and plunderers. You keep a pistol or a gun in your home because the robber is at large, and you are afraid while you sleep he will creep through the window or get through the door and make an attempt to rob your property; and because you know he is at large, and may pay you a visit, you sleep with a gun under your pillow. When all the burglars and all the robbers are put in jail, and we know they are in jail, then we will throw away our pistols and our guns. Now everybody knows that the robber—the thief—is at large; he is not only robbing domestic homes, he is robbing continents; he is robbing countries, and how do you expect, in the name of reason, for races and peoples to disarm when the thief is at large trying to get into your country, trying to get into your continent to take away your land—your birthright. The whole thing is a farce, and I trust no sensible Negro will pay any attention to it.

NEGROES MUST ARM THROUGH ORGANIZATION

I am not advising you to arm now with the things they have, I am asking you to arm through organization; arm through preparedness. You do not want to have guns and bombs just now; you have no immediate use for them, so they can throw away those things if they want in Washington on Armistice Day.[2] I am saying to the Negro people of the world, get armed with organization; get armed by coming together 400,000,000 strong. That is your weapon. Their weapon in the past has been big guns and explosive shells; your weapon must be universal organization. You are a people most favorably situated today for getting what you want through organization. Why? Because universally Negroes have a common cause; universally Negroes

[2] **Armistice Day:** On November 11, 1918, the armistice brought World War I to an end; also, any anniversary of that day.

suffer from one common disadvantage. You are not like the other people in that respect. The white people cannot organize as you are organizing. Why? Because their society is disrupted—is in chaos. Why do I say this? They are so disrupted—they are in such chaos that they have to fight against themselves—capital fighting labor, labor fighting capital. There is no common cause between capital and labor, and, therefore, they cannot get together, and will never get together until they realize the virtue of justice—the virtue of equity to all mankind. You have no fight among yourselves as between capital and labor, because all of us are laborers, therefore we need not be Socialists; we have no fight against party, because all of us are belonging to the "Suffering Party." So when it comes to organization we occupy a unique position.

England cannot organize with France, for England will be looking to rob France, and France looking to rob England, and they will be suspicious of each other. The white races will never get together. They have done so many injustices one to the other that between here and heaven they will never get together. Do you think Germany and England will ever get together? Do you think France and Germany will ever get together? They have no cause that is in common; but 400,000,000 Negroes have a cause that is in common, and that is why I pointed out to you that your strongest armament is organization, and not so much big guns and bombshells. Later on we may have to use some of those things, however, because it appears that some people cannot hear a human voice unless something is exploding nearby. Some people sleep too soundly, when it comes to a question of human rights, and you have to touch them up with something more than our ordinary human voice.

BELIEVES ARMS CONFERENCE WILL BE FIASCO

This conference on disarmament, I have said, is all a joke, and every one of them is going there to see what can be gotten. Japan to see what she can get out of America; America to see what she can get out of France; England to see what she can get out of Japan; Italy to see what she can get out of England, and the greatest vagabond will come out with the big stick. Everybody knows that; all sensible statesmen know that. They do not want any conference on disarmament, because you must arm to a certain extent. Swords are in heaven to keep the angels in good order. So since human nature is what it is, the world cannot afford to disarm. But do you know what they are getting together for? Not so much disarmament; they are getting together to form a pact by which they can subdue and further oppress the weaker peoples, who are not as strong as themselves to demand a place in this conference now to be held.

I told you during the war in my speeches throughout the length and breadth of this country and through my writings in The Negro World[3] week by week in 1916 it

[3] **The Negro World:** The newspaper created by Marcus Garvey to promote the Universal Negro Improvement Association (UNIA) until about 1933. Garvey usually wrote front page editorials focusing on black economic independence, self-awareness, and black consciousness.

was planned in England that the Negro should pay the cost of the war. You will remember (some of you) my saying that several years ago it was the determination in Europe that Africa was to be exploited to pay the cost of the war and Negroes everywhere were to be used to supply the source of revenue by which the bankrupt nations would be able to declare themselves once more solvent. Since peace was declared—since the armistice was signed—those of you who have seen the conduct of statesmen in Europe, of governments and of subsidized commercial agents, will recall that great demands have been made and are being made to commercialize the raw and mineral products of Africa, and by the spoils gained out of exploiting Africa they hope to reimburse themselves of the billions of dollars lost in the war of 1914 to 1918.

THE AIM OF EUROPEAN STATESMEN

It does not take the vision of a seer; it does not take the vision of a prophet, to see what the future will be to us, as a race, through the ambitions of the present-day statesmen of Europe. They feel that they have a divine right because of the strength of arms; because of their highly developed power to go into any part of the world and occupy it, and hold it; if that part of the world is occupied by weaker peoples. The statesmen of today believe that might makes right, and until they get that feeling out of them, until they destroy that spirit, the world cannot disarm. They fail to take into consideration, they fail to take into account, that there are 400,000,000 black men in the world today and that these 400,000,000 people are not going to allow anybody to infringe upon their rights without asking the question why. They have been playing all kinds of dodges; they have been practicing all kinds of schemes and adopting all kinds of tactics, since the armistice was signed, to keep the Negro in his old-time place, but they have failed; they cannot successfully do it. When they created the emergency, they called the Negro to battle; they placed in the Negro's hands the gun and the sword; they told him to go out and kill—kill so that the side for which you are fighting might be victorious. The Negro killed. The Negro fought his way to victory and returned the standard with honor. After the battle was won, after the victory was declared, the Negro became a puzzle. He became a puzzle to Great Britain; he became a puzzle to France; he became a puzzle to America. The American Negro was no longer wanted in active service by the American Government. What did they do? They disarmed him; they took away his pistol and his gun before he landed, so that he could not do any harm with them, and they sent him back South without any armament. What did the Frenchman[4] do? The Frenchman is puzzled up to now; they cannot send them back yet.

[4] **Frenchman:** The French armed Africans from their African colonies to fight the Germans during World War I. After the war, these Africans were not welcomed back to the colonies because their military knowledge might have proven disruptive to French rule.

All this noise they have been making about Negro soldiers being on the Rhineland, it is not because the French want the Negro to be on the Rhineland so much, but they do not know where to send him.

And do you know what they are keeping those Negroes there for? Those Negroes may never be returned to Senegal; they may never be returned to Africa. Those Negroes probably will be kept in France until they die. With the knowledge they have gained in the four years of war, they do not want those Senegalese to go back to Africa. That is why they are now on the Rhineland, and these French statesmen come and tell us it is because they love Negroes so much why they are kept in France. It is because they fear the Negroes so much why they have kept those black Senegalese on the Rhineland and in France.

A CONFERENCE OF THE "BIGGER BROTHERHOOD"

They do not know what to do. They are puzzled, and are holding conferences in France, in Switzerland, in England and now in America, and have not decided on anything. Why won't they be honest? Why won't they have a real conference? Why won't they say, "We are going to solve this great human problem; we are going to have peace forever; let us meet, whether it be in Washington, London, or Paris; come on Asia, meet us, too; come on, Africa, let us all sit around the table and let us not call this conference a disarmament conference or any such conference; let us call it a "conference of the bigger brotherhood." That is the conference the world is waiting for, and until that conference is called, it is all a farce talking about disarmament and the rest of it. Until these statesmen get ready to give Asia what is belonging to Asia, to give to Europe what is belonging to Europe, and then, above all, to give to Africa what is belonging to Africa, their conferences will be in vain.

If Great Britain will take my advice she would call a conference tomorrow morning, and say to all Englishmen leave India, leave Africa and go back to England because we want peace. If France takes my advice she will call out her white colonists from her African dominions, because so long as this injustice is perpetrated against weaker peoples there is going to be wars and rumors of wars. It is human nature and the world knows it. If you take my property, and I know it, is a different proposition, to taking my property and my not knowing it. In the past they took our property and we did not know about it, therefore we did not say anything; but they do not seem to count on the change that has come about. We know all about it now. If a man breaks into my house and steals some of my things and I do not know him, I will meet him on the street and shake hands and say, "Brother, how are you?" If he salutes me and says "Hello, how are you?" I will return it. But when I come home and find out that my property is robbed, and that he is the man who robbed my property, I am going to change my attitude. Just give me what is belonging to me. That is the situation between weaker peoples and stronger ones. They have fooled us; they have robbed us, when we did not know any better; but it is a different proposition now.

The new Negro is going to strike back or is going to die; and if David Lloyd George,[5] Briand[6] and the different statesmen believe they can assemble in Washington, in London, in Paris, or anywhere and dispose of black people's property without first consulting them they make a big mistake, because we have reared many Fochs[7] between 1914 and 1918 on the battlefields of France and Flanders. It will be a question later on of Foch meeting Foch.

Now the world of oppressed peoples have got the spirit of liberty and from far-off India we hear the cry of a free and independent India; from far-off Egypt we hear the cry of a free and independent Egypt. The Negro loves peace; the Negro likes to disarm, but the Negro says to the world, "Let us have justice; let us have equity; let us have freedom; let us have democracy indeed"; and I from Liberty Hall, on behalf of 400,000,000 Negroes, send a plea to the statesmen at Washington in their assembly on the question of disarmament, give the Negro the consideration due him; give the Hindoo the consideration due him; give the Egyptian the consideration due him; give the weaker peoples of the world the consideration due them, and let us disarm. But until then, I repeat, there will be wars and rumors of wars.

TEXT OF A TELEGRAM SENT TO THE DISARMAMENT CONFERENCE

November 11, 1921.
President and Members of the International Conference on Disarmament,
Care of Secretary of Conference, Pan-American Building,
Washington, D.C.

HONORABLE GENTLEMEN:

I salute you in the name of Democracy, and for the cause of Justice on behalf of the four hundred million Negroes of the world. Your Honorable Conference now sitting in Washington has a purpose that has been announced and advertised to the world for several months. You were called together by the President of the Democratic Republic of the United States of America to discuss the problem of armaments, the settlement of which you believe will ensure the perpetual peace of the world. As the elected spokesman of the Negro peoples of the world who desire freedom, politically, industrially, educationally, socially and religiously, as well as a full enjoyment of world democracy and a national independence all our own on the Continent of Africa, it is for me to inform you of a little slight that has been

[5] **David Lloyd George** (1863–1945): British statesman and Prime Minister of the United Kingdom from 1916–1922.

[6] **Briand:** Aristide Briand (1862–1932), French statesman and Prime Minister of France for much of World War I. Briand won the Nobel Peace Prize in 1926.

[7] **Fochs:** Ferdinand Foch (1851–1929), French soldier who became "Commander-in Chief of the Allied Armies" in 1918 during World War I. Foch was also a respected military strategist who emphasized the importance of offensive rather than defensive tactics for achieving victory in war.

shown to four hundred million Negroes who form a part of this world's population. At the Versailles Peace Conference,[8] the statesmen who gathered there made the awful mistake of legislating for the disposition of other people's lands (especially in Africa) without taking them into consideration, believing that a world peace could have been established after such a conference. The mistake is now apparent. There can be no peace among us mortals so long as the strong of humanity oppresses the weak, for in due process of time and through evolution the weak will one day turn, even like the worm, and then humanity's hope of peace will be shattered. All men have brains; some use their abilities for inventing destructive elements of warfare, such as guns, gun-powder, gas, and other destructive chemicals. The Negro for hundreds of years has attempted nothing destructive to the peace and good-will of humanity; in fact, he has not even made an attempt to make the world know that he is alive; nevertheless, like the worm, the Negro will one day turn. I humbly ask you therefore that your Honorable Conference act, not like the one at Versailles, but that you realize and appreciate the fact that the Negro is a man, and that there can be no settlement of world affairs without proper consideration being given to him with his rights. President Harding of America has but recently sounded the real cry of Democracy. He says to his own country, and I think it should be an advice to the world, "Give the Negro equality in education, in politics, in industry, because he is entitled to human rights." I humbly beg to recommend to your Honorable Conference those quoted words of President Harding. Negroes have blood, they have souls, and for the cause of Liberty they feel that the conduct of men like Alexander,[9] Hannibal,[10] Caesar, Napoleon,[11] Wellington,[12] Lafayette,[13] Garabaldi,[14] Washington, is imitable, and that peace not founded on real human justice will only be a mockery of the divine invocation, "Peace, perfect peace." I trust your Honorable Conference will not fail to take into consideration, therefore, that there are four hundred million Negroes in the world who demand Africa as their rightful heritage, even as the European claims Europe, and the Asiatic Asia. I pray that your Conference will not only be one of disarmament, but that it will be a congregation of the "Bigger Brotherhood," through which Europe will see the rights of Asia, Asia and Europe see the rights of Africa, and Africa and Asia see the rights of Europe and accordingly give every race and nation their due, and let there be peace indeed. On behalf of the four hundred million Negroes of the world not represented at your Honorable Conference.

[8] **Versailles Peace Conference:** Also called the Paris Peace Conference (1919–1920), it was organized by Allied Powers of World War I to negotiate the peace treaties between themselves and the Central Powers after their defeat.

[9] **Alexander:** Alexander the Great (356–323 B.C.E.), Greek military commander.

[10] **Hannibal** (247–183 B.C.E.): Carthaginian statesman, politician, and general.

[11] **Napoleon Bonaparte** (1769–1821): Emperor of France.

[12] **Arthur Wellesley, 1st Duke of Wellington** (1769–1852): Irish-born British soldier and statesman.

[13] **Marquis de Lafayette** (1757–1834): French aristocrat and soldier who aided the United States in the Revolutionary War.

[14] **Giuseppe Garibaldi** (1807–1882): Italian soldier whose campaigns led to a unified Italy.

I have the honor to be
Your obedient servant,
MARCUS GARVEY,
President General of the Universal Negro Improvement Association and First Provisional President of Africa, New York City.

REPLY

November 17, 1921.
Conference of the Limitation of Armament,
Secretariat General.

SIR: I am directed by the Secretary General, the Chairman of the Conference, to acknowledge the receipt of your communication, which has been read with attention.

I am charged to express to you his appreciation of the interest and support which you have been so good to evince.

I am, sir,
Yours very truly,
T. G. W. PAUL,
For the Secretary General.
Mr. Marcus Garvey, President-General Universal Negro Improvement Association, 56 West 135th Street, New York.

—1921, 1923

Zora Neale Hurston 1891–1960

An influential and prolific African American writer, folklorist, and anthropologist, Zora Neale Hurston is the author of four novels, including *Their Eyes Were Watching God* (1937); two significant books of folklore and voodoo rituals, including *Mules and Men* (1935); an acclaimed autobiography, *Dust Tracks on a Road* (1942); and numerous short stories, plays, poems, essays, and journal articles.

Hurston grew up in Eatonville, Florida, one of the nation's first black municipalities. This experience of living in a self-governing black community had a profound impact on her work both thematically and politically, and stories such as "Sweat" and "Spunk" are set in this town. Hurston moved to New York in 1925 and enrolled at Barnard College, where she studied under the "father of modern anthropology," Franz Boas. She was also a major voice in the New Negro Renaissance. As a younger member of the Renaissance, Hurston, along with Langston Hughes and Wallace Thurman, challenged the established leaders, W. E. B. DuBois, Charles S. Johnson, James Weldon Johnson, Jessie Fauset, and Alain Locke. Turning to the black folk tradition for inspiration,

Hurston gave voice to a modern and urbane use of folklore. For Hurston and the younger members of the New Negro Renaissance, the black folk tradition with its unique dialect, spontaneity, and populist tendencies was an ideal medium to articulate the desires of the New Negro; the folk tradition would also, perhaps, prevent racial and class assimilation and be an effective voice of protest.

In 1937, Hurston published what many consider to be her best work, *Their Eyes Were Watching God.* Portraying the life and three marriages of its heroine Janie Crawford, the novel projects not only a new image of black women and a self-sufficient black community but also an innovative understanding of black folk vernacular and its rich poetic resources. Her novel was greeted initially with mixed reviews. The strongest criticism came from black male critics who accused Hurston of presenting an idyllic view of black folk life. Richard Wright's well-known review, printed in the *New Masses,* was the most severe in its assessment. Wright charged Hurston with "voluntarily [continuing] in her novel the tradition which was forced upon the Negro in the theatre, that is, the minstrel technique that makes the 'white folks' laugh." Similar derogatory commentary by Langston Hughes, Nathan Huggins, Wallace Thurman, and Dwight Turner portrayed Hurston as an opportunist who pandered to wealthy whites to further her own career.

Hurston's popularity began to wane in the 1940s, declining more so in the 1950s with her controversial political statements supporting segregation. Hurston died in 1960, an impoverished and virtually forgotten writer. In the 1970s, with the rise of feminist and African American studies, Hurston's work had an astonishing revival, led by novelist Alice Walker and literary critic Robert Hemenway. All of Hurston's published work is currently available and the majority of her unpublished work is also in the process of being made publicly available. The 2003 publication of Carla Kaplan's *Zora Neale Hurston: A Life in Letters* also provides new perspective into the life of this fascinating writer.

As the selection included here, "How It Feels to Be Colored Me," illustrates, Hurston was an effective social commentator not only in her well-known novel but also in her prose essays. Hurston's brand of social criticism is much more subtle than that of Marcus Garvey, Walter White, or Richard Wright. Still, she makes her points clear through depictions of the traumatic effects of racism on a young psyche. Discrimination does not make Hurston feel tragic, but it does at times make her feel astonished: "How *can* any deny themselves the pleasure of my company? It's beyond me." Hurston manages to convey the harm of racism, but throughout the short piece she maintains a humorous, reflective, and understated tone of social commentary and irony.

Further Reading Robert E. Hemingway, *Zora Neale Hurston: A Literary Biography* (1977); Zora Neale Hurston, *Folklore, Memoirs, and Other Writings* (1995); Carla Kaplan, *Zora Neale Hurston: A Life in Letters* (2003); Alice Walker, ed., *I Love Myself When I am Laughing. . . and Then Again When I am Looking Mean and Impressive: A Zora Neale Hurston Reader* (1979).

—Delia Konzett, University of New Hampshire

How It Feels to Be Colored Me

I AM COLORED but I offer nothing in the way of extenuating circumstances except the fact that I am the only Negro in the United States whose grandfather on the mother's side was *not* an Indian chief.

I remember the very day that I became colored. Up to my thirteenth year I lived in the little Negro town of Eatonville, Florida. It is exclusively a colored town. The only white people I knew passed through the town going to or coming from Orlando. The native whites rode dusty horses, the Northern tourists chugged down the sandy village road in automobiles. The town knew the Southerners and never stopped cane chewing when they passed. But the Northerners were something else again. They were peered at cautiously from behind curtains by the timid. The more venturesome would come out on the porch to watch them go past and got just as much pleasure out of the tourists as the tourists got out of the village.

The front porch might seem a daring place for the rest of the town, but it was a gallery seat for me. My favorite place was atop the gate-post. Proscenium box[1] for a born first-nighter.[2] Not only did I enjoy the show, but I didn't mind the actors knowing that I liked it. I usually spoke to them in passing. I'd wave at them and when they returned my salute, I would say something like this: "Howdy-do-well-I-thank-you-where-you-goin'?" Usually automobile or the horse paused at this, and after a queer exchange of compliments, I would probably "go a piece of the way" with them, as we say in farthest Florida. If one of my family happened to come to the front in time to see me, of course negotiations would be rudely broken off. But even so, it is clear that I was the first "welcome-to-our-state" Floridian, and I hope the Miami Chamber of Commerce will please take notice.

During this period, white people differed from colored to me only in that they rode through town and never lived there. They liked to hear me "speak pieces" and sing and wanted to see me dance the parse-me-la, and gave me generously of their small silver for doing these things, which seemed strange to me for I wanted to do them so much that I needed bribing to stop. Only they didn't know it. The colored people gave no dimes. They deplored any joyful tendencies in me, but I was their Zora nevertheless. I belonged to them, to the nearby hotels, to the county—everybody's Zora.

But changes came in the family when I was thirteen, and I was sent to school in Jacksonville. I left Eatonville, the town of the oleanders, as Zora. When I disembarked from the river-boat at Jacksonville, she was no more. It seemed that I had suffered a sea change. I was not Zora of Orange County any more, I was now a little colored girl. I found it out in certain ways. In my heart as well as in the mirror, I became a fast brown—warranted not to rub nor run.

---

[1] **Proscenium box:** Box at the front of the auditorium, closest to the stage.

[2] **first-nighter:** One who attends a play on the night it is first produced on stage.

But I am not tragically colored. There is no great sorrow dammed up in my soul, nor lurking behind my eyes. I do not mind at all. I do not belong to the sobbing school of Negrohood who hold that nature somehow has given them a lowdown dirty deal and whose feelings are all hurt about it. Even in the helter-skelter skirmish that is my life, I have seen that the world is to the strong regardless of a little pigmentation more or less. No, I do not weep at the world—I am too busy sharpening my oyster knife.

Someone is always at my elbow reminding me that I am the granddaughter of slaves. It fails to register depression with me. Slavery is sixty years in the past. The operation was successful and the patient is doing well, thank you. The terrible struggle that made me an American out of a potential slave said "On the line!" The Reconstruction said "Get set!"; and the generation before said "Go!" I am off to a flying start and I must not halt in the stretch to look behind and weep. Slavery is the price I paid for civilization, and the choice was not with me. It is a bully adventure and worth all that I have paid through my ancestors for it. No one on earth ever had a greater chance for glory. The world to be won and nothing to be lost. It is thrilling to think—to know that for any act of mine, I shall get twice as much praise or twice as much blame. It is quite exciting to hold the center of the national stage, with the spectators not knowing whether to laugh or to weep.

The position of my white neighbor is much more difficult. No brown specter pulls up a chair beside me when I sit down to eat. No dark ghost thrusts its leg against mine in bed. The game of keeping what one has is never so exciting as the game of getting.

I do not always feel colored. Even now I often achieve the unconscious Zora of Eatonville before the Hegira.[3] I feel most colored when I am thrown against a sharp white background.

For instance at Barnard. "Beside the waters of the Hudson" I feel my race. Among the thousand white persons, I am a dark rock surged upon, and overswept, but through it all, I remain myself. When covered by the waters, I am; and the ebb but reveals me again.

Sometimes it is the other way around. A white person is set down in our midst, but the contrast is just as sharp for me. For instance, when I sit in the drafty basement that is The New World Cabaret[4] with a white person, my color comes. We enter chatting about any little nothing that we have in common and are seated by the jazz waiters. In the abrupt way that jazz orchestras have, this one plunges into a number. It loses no time in circumlocutions, but gets right down to business. It constricts the thorax and splits the heart with its tempo and narcotic harmonies.

[3] **Hegira:** Reference to the flight of Muhammad from Mecca to Medina in 622 A.D., on which point Muslim chronology is based. Also refers to any forced flight or journey.

[4] **New World Cabaret:** Popular nightclub in 1920s Harlem.

This orchestra grows rambunctious, rears on its hind legs and attacks the tonal veil with primitive fury, rending it, clawing it until it breaks through to the jungle beyond. I follow those heathen—follow them exultingly. I dance wildly inside myself; I yell within, I whoop; I shake my assegai[5] above my head, I hurl it true to the mark *yeeeeooww!* I am in the jungle and living in the jungle way. My face is painted red and yellow and my body is painted blue. My pulse is throbbing like a war drum. I want to slaughter something—give pain, give death to what, I do not know. But the piece ends. The men of the orchestra wipe their lips and rest their fingers. I creep back slowly to the veneer we call civilization with the last tone and find the white friend sitting motionless in his seat, smoking calmly.

"Good music they have here," he remarks, drumming the table with his fingertips.

Music. The great blobs of purple and red emotion have not touched him. He has only heard what I felt. He is far away and I see him but dimly across the ocean and the continent that have fallen between us. He is so pale with his whiteness then and I am *so* colored.

At certain times I have no race, I am *me*. When I set my hat at a certain angle and saunter down Seventh Avenue, Harlem City, feeling as snooty as the lions in front of the Forty-Second Street Library, for instance. So far as my feelings are concerned, Peggy Hopkins Joyce[6] on the Boule Mich[7] with her gorgeous raiment, stately carriage, knees knocking together in a most aristocratic manner, has nothing on me. The cosmic Zora emerges. I belong to no race nor time. I am the eternal feminine with its string of beads.

I have no separate feeling about being an American citizen and colored. I am merely a fragment of the Great Soul that surges within the boundaries. My country, right or wrong.

Sometimes, I feel discriminated against, but it does not make me angry. It merely astonishes me. How *can* any deny themselves the pleasure of my company? It's beyond me.

But in the main, I feel like a brown bag of miscellany propped against a wall. Against a wall in company with other bags, white, red and yellow. Pour out the contents, and there is discovered a jumble of small things priceless and worthless. A first-water diamond, an empty spool, bits of broken glass, lengths of string, a key to a door long since crumbled away, a rusty knife-blade, old shoes saved for a road that never was and never will be, a nail bent under the weight of things too heavy for any nail, a dried flower or two still a little fragrant. In your hand is the brown bag. On the ground before you is the jumble it held—so much like the

[5] **assegai:** A spear.

[6] **Peggy Hopkins Joyce** (1893–1957): American actress known for her marriages to wealthy men and lavish lifestyle.

[7] **Boule Mich:** The Boulevard Saint-Michel, a major street in the Latin Quarter of Paris near the Sorbonne University—frequented by Americans in Paris.

jumble in the bags, could they be emptied, that all might be dumped in a single heap and the bags refilled without altering the content of any greatly. A bit of colored glass more or less would not matter. Perhaps that is how the Great Stuffer of Bags filled them in the first place—who knows?

—1928

Jean Toomer was light-skinned enough to "pass" for white but chose instead to ally himself with his African American heritage while writing his work *Cane*.

Jean Toomer 1894–1967

Jean Toomer was born Nathan Pinchback Toomer to Nina Pinchback and Nathan Toomer in Washington, D.C. In 1896, he and his mother returned to live with her parents after his father's desertion. He was called Eugene, after his godfather, to avoid any reference to Nathan Toomer. Toomer moved with his mother to New York after her remarriage in 1906, but returned to his grandparents' house three years later when his mother died. He lived first in predominantly white neighborhoods and later in a black neighborhood and attended mostly black schools; he could "pass" for white but deeply identified with his African American heritage. He felt that he had intimate knowledge of both groups and resisted any singular racial identity.

Although Toomer wrote poetry, drama, stories, novels, essays, epigrams, and autobiography, he is known mainly for *Cane* (1923), a multi-genre volume that strongly influenced New Negro Renaissance writers in the 1920s and Black Arts writers in the 1960s—despite being out of print for forty years in between. Like other modernist works, *Cane* employs a collage structure, juxtaposing poems, stories, and quasi-dramatic pieces to suggest fragmentation, dislocation, and loss of authority, modern experiences that could be both destructive and liberating. The book explores the effects of modernity on African Americans who migrated from the South to the North early in the century and is structured in three parts: part one represents the rural South, part two the urban industrial North, and part three, "Kabnis," treats a Northern-reared black man like Toomer, who discovers both his rich cultural roots and the history of racial violence when he goes to teach in the South.

Toomer is most often thought of as a poet since even his prose is lyrical and elliptical. He associated poetry with his African and African American ancestry, and *Cane* tracks the loss of this sustaining "song" as blacks move from their ancestral lands in the rural South and become modernized. Poems like "November Cotton Flower" are written in conventional ballad or sonnet form and embody the songlike qualities that Toomer associated with the black past. In contrast, free-verse poems like "Portrait in Georgia" tend to depict African Americans as victims of violence and cultural dislocation. Even his stories focus on the role of song in African American life. "Blood-Burning Moon" incorporates poetry, creating a tension between the ancestral voice of the poetry and the alienated or abused characters of the stories.

Toomer wrote *Cane* during a brief period between 1918 and 1922. By the time the book was published, he had shifted his interest from racial identity to spirituality and no longer wanted to be defined by any racial category. He became a follower of the spiritual leader G. I. Gurdjieff; he led Gurdjieff workshops in the United States and established a commune. Throughout his life he was a spiritual seeker, joining the Society of Friends (Quakers), traveling to India, undergoing Jungian analysis, and investigating Dianetics (Church of Scientology). Most of his later writings reflect these interests and are extremely didactic in nature; these works were not well received, so his reputation mainly rests on *Cane*.

"Blood-Burning Moon" and "Portrait in Georgia," the two pieces featured here, both are from Part One of *Cane*, set in the South. They depict the on-going violence against African American men and women that would lead to the more militant activism of writers such as Marcus Garvey and (eventually) Malcolm X, who said, famously, "I don't call it violence. When it's self-defense, I call it intelligence."

Further Reading Geneviève Fabre and Michel Feith, eds., *Jean Toomer and the Harlem Renaissance* (2001); Karen Jackson Ford, *Split-Gut Song: Jean Toomer and the Poetics of Modernity* (2005); Cynthia Earl Kerman and Richard Eldridge, *The Lives of Jean Toomer: A Hunger for Wholeness* (1987); Charles Scruggs and Lee Vandemarr, *Jean Toomer and the Terrors of American History* (1998).

—*Karen Ford, University of Oregon*

From Cane

Portrait in Georgia

Hair—braided chestnut,
  coiled like a lyncher's rope,
Eyes—fagots,[1]
Lips—old scars, or the first red blisters,
Breath—the last sweet scent of cane,
And her slim body, white as the ash
  of black flesh after flame.

—1923

Blood-Burning Moon

1

Up from the skeleton stone walls, up from the rotting floor boards and the solid hand-hewn beams of oak of the pre-war cotton factory, dusk came. Up from the dusk the full moon came. Glowing like a fired pine-knot, it illumined the great door

[1] **fagots:** A bundle of sticks used for fuel.

and soft showered the Negro shanties aligned along the single street of factory town. The full moon in the great door was an omen. Negro women improvised songs against its spell.

Louisa sang as she came over the crest of the hill from the white folks' kitchen. Her skin was the color of oak leaves on young trees in fall. Her breasts, firm and up-pointed like ripe acorns. And her singing had the low murmur of winds in fig trees. Bob Stone, younger son of the people she worked for, loved her. By the way the world reckons things, he had won her. By measure of that warm glow which came into her mind at thought of him, he had won her. Tom Burwell, whom the whole town called Big Boy, also loved her. But working in the fields all day, and far away from her, gave him no chance to show it. Though often enough of evenings he had tried to. Some-how, he never got along. Strong as he was with hands upon the ax or plow, he found it difficult to hold her. Or so he thought. But the fact was that he held her to factory town more firmly than he thought for. His black balanced, and pulled against, the white of Stone, when she thought of them. And her mind was vaguely upon them as she came over the crest of the hill, coming from the white folks' kitchen. As she sang softly at the evil face of the full moon.

A strange stir was in her. Indolently, she tried to fix upon Bob or Tom as the cause of it. To meet Bob in the canebrake, as she was going to do an hour or so later, was nothing new. And Tom's proposal which she felt on its way to her could be in-definitely put off. Separately, there was no unusual significance to either one. But for some reason, they jumbled when her eyes gazed vacantly at the rising moon. And from the jumble came the stir that was strangely within her. Her lips trembled. The slow rhythm of her song grew agitant and restless. Rusty black and tan spotted hounds, lying in the dark corners of porches or prowling around back yards, put their noses in the air and caught its tremor. They began plaintively to yelp and howl. Chickens woke up and cackled. Intermittently, all over the countryside dogs barked and roosters crowed as if heralding a weird dawn or some ungodly awakening. The women sang lustily. Their songs were cotton-wads to stop their ears. Louisa came down into factory town and sank wearily upon the step before her home. The moon was rising towards a thick cloud-bank which soon would hide it.

Red nigger moon. Sinner!
Blood-burning moon. Sinner!
Come out that fact'ry door.

2

Up from the deep dusk of a cleared spot on the edge of the forest a mellow glow arose and spread fan-wise into the low-hanging heavens. And all around the air was heavy with the scent of boiling cane. A large pile of cane-stalks lay like ribboned shadows upon the ground. A mule, harnessed to a pole, trudged lazily round and round the pivot of the grinder. Beneath a swaying oil lamp, a Negro alternately whipped out at the mule, and fed cane-stalks to the grinder. A fat boy waddled pails of fresh ground juice between the grinder and the boiling stove. Steam came from the copper boiling pan. The scent of cane came from the copper pan and drenched the forest and the hill that sloped to factory town, beneath its fragrance. It drenched the men in circle seated around the stove. Some of them chewed at the white pulp of stalks, but there was no need for them to, if all they wanted was to taste the cane. One tasted it in factory town. And from factory town one could see the soft haze thrown by the glowing stove upon the low-hanging heavens.

Old David Georgia stirred the thickening syrup[1] with a long ladle, and ever so often drew it off. Old David Georgia tended his stove and told tales about the white folks, about moonshining and cotton picking, and about sweet nigger gals, to the men who sat there about his stove to listen to him. Tom Burwell chewed cane-stalk and laughed with the others till some one mentioned Louisa. Till some one said something about Louisa and Bob Stone, about the silk stockings she must have gotten from him. Blood ran up Tom's neck hotter than the glow that flooded from the stove. He sprang up. Glared at the men and said, "She's my gal." Will Manning laughed. Tom strode over to him. Yanked him up and knocked him to the ground. Several of Manning's friends got up to fight for him. Tom whipped out a long knife and would have cut them to shreds if they hadnt ducked into the woods. Tom had had enough. He nodded to Old David Georgia and swung down the path to factory town. Just then, the dogs started barking and the roosters began to crow. Tom felt funny. Away from the fight, away from the stove, chill got to him. He shivered. He shuddered when he saw the full moon rising towards the cloud-bank. He who didnt give a godam for the fears of old women. He forced his mind to fasten on Louisa. Bob Stone. Better not be. He turned into the street and saw Louisa sitting before her home. He went towards her, ambling, touched the brim of a marvelously shaped, spotted, felt hat, said he wanted to say something to her, and then found that he didnt know what he had to say, or if he did, that he couldnt say it. He shoved his big fists in his overalls, grinned, and started to move off.

"Youall want me, Tom?"

"Thats what us wants, sho, Louisa."

"Well, here I am—"

"An here I is, but that aint ahelpin none, all th same."

"You wanted to say something? . ."

"I did that, sho. But words is like th spots on dice: no matter how y fumbles em, there's times when they jes wont come. I dunno why. Seems like th love I feels fo yo done stole m tongue. I got it now. Whee! Louisa, honey, I oughtnt tell y, I feel I

[1] **syrup:** The Depression of 1921 caused prices for cane syrup to drop low and shipping rates to increase, so many farmers had an unsellable surplus that was good only for use-value.

oughtnt cause yo is young an goes t church an I has had other gals, but Louisa I sho do love y. Lil gal, Ise watched y from them first days when youall sat right here befo yo door befo th well an sang sometimes in a way that like t broke m heart. Ise carried y with me into th fields, day after day, an after that, an I sho can plow when yo is there, an I can pick cotton. Yassur! Come near beatin Barlo yesterday. I sho did. Yassur! An next year if ole Stone'll trust me, I'll have a farm. My own. My bales will buy yo what y gets from white folks now. Silk stockings an purple dresses—course I dont believe what some folks been whisperin as t how y gets them things now. White folks always did do for niggers what they likes. An they jes cant help alikin yo, Louisa. Bob Stone likes y. Course he does. But not th way folks is awhisperin. Does he, hon?"

"I dont know what you mean, Tom."

"Course y dont. Ise already cut two niggers. Had t hon, t tell em so. Niggers always tryin t make somethin out a nothin. An then besides, white folks aint up t them tricks so much nowadays. Godam better not be. Leastawise not with yo. Cause I wouldnt stand f it. Nassur."

"What would you do, Tom?"

"Cut him jes like I cut a nigger."

"No, Tom—"

"I said I would an there aint no mo to it. But that aint th talk f now. Sing, honey Louisa, an while I'm listenin t y I'll be makin love."

Tom took her hand in his. Against the tough thickness of his own, hers felt soft and small. His huge body slipped down to the step beside her. The full moon sank upward into the deep purple of the cloud-bank. An old woman brought a lighted lamp and hung it on the common well whose bulky shadow squatted in the middle of the road, opposite Tom and Louisa. The old woman lifted the well-lid, took hold the chain, and began drawing up the heavy bucket. As she did so, she sang. Figures shifted, restlesslike, between lamp and window in the front rooms of the shanties. Shadows of the figures fought each other on the gray dust of the road. Figures raised the windows and joined the old woman in song. Louisa and Tom, the whole street, singing:

> Red nigger moon. Sinner!
> Blood-burning moon. Sinner!
> Come out that fact'ry door.

3

Bob Stone sauntered from his veranda out into the gloom of fir trees and magnolias. The clear white of his skin paled, and the flush of his cheeks turned purple. As if to balance this outer change, his mind became consciously a white man's. He passed the house with its huge open hearth which, in the days of slavery, was the plantation cookery. He saw Louisa bent over that hearth. He went in as a master should and took her. Direct, honest, bold. None of this sneaking that he had to go through now. The contrast was repulsive to him. His family had lost ground. Hell no, his family still owned the niggers, practically. Damned if they did, or he wouldnt have to duck around so. What would they think if they knew? His mother? His sister? He shouldnt mention them, shouldnt think of them in this connection. There in the dusk he blushed at doing so. Fellows about town were all right, but how about his friends up North? He could see them incredible, repulsed. They didnt know. The thought first made him laugh. Then, with their eyes still upon him, he began to feel embarrassed. He felt the need of explaining things to them. Explain hell. They wouldnt understand, and moreover, who ever heard of a Southerner getting on his knees to any Yankee, or anyone. No sir. He was going to see Louisa to-night, and love her. She was lovely—in her way. Nigger way. What way was that? Damned if he knew. Must know. He'd known her long enough to know. Was there something about niggers that you couldnt know? Listening to them at church didnt tell you anything. Looking at them didnt tell you anything. Talking to them didnt tell you anything—unless it was gossip, unless they wanted to talk. Of course, about farming, and licker, and craps—but those werent nigger. Nigger was something more. How much more? Something to be afraid of, more? Hell no. Who ever heard of being afraid of a nigger? Tom Burwell. Cartwell had told him that Tom went with Louisa after she reached home. No sir. No nigger had ever been with his girl. He'd like to see one try. Some position for him to be in. Him, Bob Stone, of the old Stone family, in a scrap with a nigger over a nigger girl. In the good old days … Ha! Those were the days. His family had lost ground. Not so much, though. Enough for him to have to cut through old Lemon's canefield by way of the woods, that he might meet her. She was worth it. Beautiful nigger gal. Why nigger? Why not, just gal? No, it was because she was nigger that he went to her. Sweet … The scent of boiling cane came to him. Then he saw the rich glow of the stove. He heard the voices of the men circled around it. He was about to skirt the clearing when he heard his own name mentioned. He stopped. Quivering. Leaning against a tree, he listened.

"Bad nigger. Yassur, he sho is one bad nigger when he gets started."

"Tom Burwell's been on th gang three times fo cuttin men."

"What y think he's agwine t do t Bob Stone?"

"Dunno yet. He aint found out. When he does—Baby!"

"Aint no tellin."

"Young Stone aint no quitter an I ken tell y that. Blood of th old uns in his veins."

"Thats right. He'll scrap, sho."

"Be gettin too hot f niggers round this away."

"Shut up, nigger. Y dont know what y talkin bout."

Bob Stone's ears burned as though he had been holding them over the stove. Sizzling heat welled up within him. His feet felt as if they rested on red-hot coals.

They stung him to quick movement. He circled the fringe of the glowing. Not a twig cracked beneath his feet. He reached the path that led to factory town. Plunged furiously down it. Halfway along, a blindness within him veered him aside. He crashed into the bordering canebrake. Cane leaves cut his face and lips. He tasted blood. He threw himself down and dug his fingers in the ground. The earth was cool. Cane-roots took the fever from his hands. After a long while, or so it seemed to him, the thought came to him that it must be time to see Louisa. He got to his feet and walked calmly to their meeting place. No Louisa. Tom Burwell had her. Veins in his forehead bulged and distended. Saliva moistened the dried blood on his lips. He bit down on his lips. He tasted blood. Not his own blood; Tom Burwell's blood. Bob drove through the cane and out again upon the road. A hound swung down the path before him towards factory town. Bob couldnt see it. The dog loped aside to let him pass. Bob's blind rushing made him stumble over it. He fell with a thud that dazed him. The hound yelped. Answering yelps came from all over the countryside. Chickens cackled. Roosters crowed, heralding the bloodshot eyes of southern awakening. Singers in the town were silenced. They shut their windows down. Palpitant between the rooster crows, a chill hush settled upon the huddled forms of Tom and Louisa. A figure rushed from the shadow and stood before them. Tom popped to his feet.

"Whats y want?"

"I'm Bob Stone."

"Yassur—an I'm Tom Burwell. Whats y want?"

Bob lunged at him. Tom side-stepped, caught him by the shoulder, and flung him to the ground. Straddled him.

"Let me up."

"Yassur—but watch yo doins, Bob Stone."

A few dark figures, drawn by the sound of scuffle, stood about them. Bob sprang to his feet.

"Fight like a man, Tom Burwell, an I'll lick y."

Again he lunged. Tom side-stepped and flung him to the ground. Straddled him.

"Get off me, you godam nigger you."

"Yo sho has started somethin now. Get up."

Tom yanked him up and began hammering at him. Each blow sounded as if it smashed into a precious, irreplaceable soft something. Beneath them, Bob staggered back. He reached in his pocket and whipped out a knife.

"Thats my game, sho."

Blue flash, a steel blade slashed across Bob Stone's throat. He had a sweetish sick feeling. Blood began to flow. Then he felt a sharp twitch of pain. He let his knife drop. He slapped one hand against his neck. He pressed the other on top of his head as if to hold it down. He groaned. He turned, and staggered towards the crest of the hill in the direction of white town. Negroes who had seen the fight slunk into their homes and blew the lamps out. Louisa, dazed, hysterical, refused to go indoors. She slipped, crumbled, her body loosely propped against the woodwork of the well. Tom Burwell leaned against it. He seemed rooted there.

Bob reached Broad Street. White men rushed up to him. He collapsed in their arms.

"Tom Burwell...."

White men like ants upon a forage rushed about. Except for the taut hum of their moving, all was silent. Shotguns, revolvers, rope, kerosene, torches. Two high-powered cars with glaring search-lights. They came together. The taut hum rose to a low roar. Then nothing could be heard but the flop of their feet in the thick dust of the road. The moving body of their silence preceded them over the crest of the hill into factory town. It flattened the Negroes beneath it. It rolled to the wall of the factory, where it stopped. Tom knew that they were coming. He couldnt move. And then he saw the search-lights of the two cars glaring down on him. A quick shock went through him. He stiffened. He started to run. A yell went up from the mob. Tom wheeled about and faced them. They poured down on him. They swarmed. A large man with dead-white face and flabby cheeks came to him and almost jabbed a gun-barrel through his guts.

"Hands behind y, nigger."

Tom's wrists were bound. The big man shoved him to the well. Burn him over it, and when the woodwork caved in, his body would drop to the bottom. Two deaths for a godam nigger. Louisa was driven back. The mob pushed in. Its pressure, its momentum was too great. Drag him to the factory. Wood and stakes already there. Tom moved in the direction indicated. But they had to drag him. They reached the great door. Too many to get in there. The mob divided and flowed around the walls to either side. The big man shoved him through the door. The mob pressed in from the sides. Taut humming. No words. A stake was sunk into the ground. Rotting floor boards piled around it. Kerosene poured on the rotting floor boards. Tom bound to the stake. His breast was bare. Nails' scratches let little lines of blood trickle down and mat into the hair. His face, his eyes were set and stony. Except for irregular breathing, one would have thought him already dead. Torches were flung onto the pile. A great flare muffled in black smoke shot upward. The mob yelled. The mob was silent. Now Tom could be seen within the flames. Only his head, erect, lean, like a blackened stone. Stench of burning flesh soaked the air. Tom's eyes popped. His head settled downward. The mob yelled. Its yell echoed against the skeleton stone walls and sounded like a hundred yells. Like a hundred mobs yelling. Its yell thudded against the thick front wall and fell back. Ghost of a yell slipped through the flames and out the great door of the factory. It fluttered like a dying thing down the single street of factory town. Louisa, upon the step before her home, did not hear it, but her eyes opened slowly. They saw the full moon glowing in the great door. The full moon, an evil thing, an omen, soft showering the homes of folks she knew. Where were they, these people? She'd sing, and perhaps they'd come out and join her. Perhaps Tom Burwell would come. At any rate, the full moon in the great door was an omen which she must sing to:

Red nigger moon. Sinner!
Blood-burning moon. Sinner!
Come out that fact'ry door.

—1923

Walter White 1893–1955

Walter White was one of the most important writers, political leaders, and civil rights activists of the early twentieth century. White grew up in Atlanta, Georgia, and began his career of activism shortly after his 1916 graduation from Atlanta University, when he spearheaded a protest against the Atlanta Board of Education's plan to drop seventh grade education for black students in order to finance the building of a new white high school. He went on to become the acting executive secretary of the NAACP (the National Association for the Advancement of Colored People) in 1929 and to lead its fight for the passage of anti-lynching legislation. Born with fair skin and blue eyes, White used his ability to "pass" for white to investigate over forty deaths due to lynching and race riots in the South. White orchestrated massive support in Congress for an anti-lynching law, but the law was defeated by a slim margin. White served as executive secretary of the NAACP until 1955 and led other successful reforms in desegregating the military and schools.

White wrote numerous articles, a newspaper column, two novels—*Fire in the Flint* (1924) and *Flight* (1926)—several works of nonfiction and an autobiography, *A Man Called White* (1948). In "I Investigate Lynching" White does not dwell on the bloody details of lynching, but instead focuses on the blatant refusal of white politicians and lawmakers to prosecute the perpetrators of these crimes. In so doing he illustrates that writing itself can be a form of activism, an instrument of political reform and social change.

Further Reading Kenneth R. Janken, "Civil Rights and Socializing in the Harlem Renaissance: Walter White and the Fictionalization of the 'New Negro' in Georgia," *Georgia Historical Quarterly* 80 (1996): 817-34; Kenneth R. Janken, *White: The Biography of Walter White, Mr. NAACP* (2003); Walter White, *A Man Called White* (1948).

I Investigate Lynching

Nothing contributes so much to the continued life of an investigator of lynchings and his tranquil possession of all his limbs as the obtuseness of the lynchers themselves. Like most boastful people who practice direct action when it involves no personal risk, they just can't help talk about their deeds to any person who manifests even the slightest interest in them.

Most lynchings take place in small towns and rural regions where the natives know practically nothing of what is going on outside their own immediate neighborhoods. Newspapers, books, magazines, theatres, visitors and other vehicles for the transmission of information and ideas are usually as strange among them as drypoint etchings. But those who live in so sterile an atmosphere usually esteem their own perspicacity in about the same degree as they are isolated from the world of ideas. They gabble on *ad infinitum*, apparently unable to keep from talking.

In any American village, North or South, East or West, there is no problem which cannot be solved in half an hour by the morons who lounge about the village store. World peace, or the lack of it, the tariff, sex, religion, the settlement of the war debts, short skirts, Prohibition, the carryings-on of the younger generation, the superior moral rectitude of country people over city dwellers (with a wistful eye on urban sins)—all these controversial subjects are disposed of quickly and finally by the bucolic wise men. When to their isolation is added an emotional fixation such as the rural South has on the Negro, one can sense the atmosphere from which spring the Heflins,[1] the Ku Kluxers, the two-gun Bible-beaters, the lynchers and the anti-evolutionists. And one can see why no great amount of cleverness or courage is needed to acquire information in such a forlorn place about the latest lynching.

Professor Earle Fiske Young of the University of Southern California recently analyzed the lynching returns from fourteen Southern States for thirty years. He found that in counties of less than 10,000 people there was a lynching rate of 3.2 per 100,000 of population; that in those of from 10,000 to 20,000 the rate dropped to 2.4; that in those of from 20,000 to 30,000, it was 2.1 per cent; that in those of from 30,000 to 40,000, it was 1.7, and that thereafter it kept on going down until in counties with from 300,000 to 800,000 population it was only 0.05.

Of the forty-one lynchings and eight race riots I have investigated for the National Association for the Advancement of Colored People during the past ten years all of the lynchings and seven of the riots occurred in rural or semi-rural communities. The towns ranged in population from around one hundred to ten thousand or so.

[1] **Heflins:** James Thomas Heflin (1869–1951), a United States Senator from Alabama from 1920–1930. Heflin was famous for his racist views, and in some of his political campaigns he openly boasted about having shot and wounded a black man who confronted him on a streetcar in 1908. He would later publicly oppose the pardoning of the "Scottsboro Boys" in their Alabama rape case.

The lynchings were not difficult to inquire into because of the fact already noted that those who perpetrated them were in nearly every instance simple-minded and easily fooled individuals. On but three occasions were suspicions aroused by my too definite questions or by informers who had seen me in other places. These three times I found it rather desirable to disappear slightly in advance of reception committees imbued with the desire to make an addition to the lynching record. One other time the possession of a light skin and blue eyes (though I consider myself a colored man) almost cost me my life when (it was during the Chicago race riots in 1919) a Negro shot at me thinking me to be a white man.

II

In 1918 a Negro woman, about to give birth to a child, was lynched with almost unmentionable brutality along with ten men in Georgia. I reached the scene shortly after the butchery and while excitement yet ran high. It was a prosperous community. Forests of pine trees gave rich returns in turpentine, tar and pitch. The small towns where the farmers and turpentine hands traded were fat and rich. The main streets of the largest of these towns were well paved and lighted. The stores were well stocked. The white inhabitants belonged to the class of Georgia crackers—lanky, slow of movement and of speech, long-necked, with small eyes set close together, and skin tanned by the hot sun to a reddish-yellow hue.

As I was born in Georgia and spent twenty years of my life there, my accent is sufficiently Southern to enable me to talk with Southerners and not arouse their suspicion that I am an outsider. (In the rural South hatred of Yankees is not much less than hatred of Negroes.) On the morning of my arrival in the town I casually dropped into the store of one of the general merchants who, I had been informed, had been one of the leaders of the mob. After making a small purchase I engaged the merchant in conversation. There was, at the time, no other customer in the store. We spoke of the weather, the possibility of good crops in the Fall, the political situation, the latest news from the war in Europe. As his manner became more and more friendly I ventured to mention guardedly the recent lynchings.

Instantly he became cautious—until I hinted that I had great admiration for the manly spirit the men of the town had exhibited. I mentioned the newspaper accounts I had read and confessed that I had never been so fortunate as to see a lynching. My words or tone seemed to disarm his suspicions. He offered me a box on which to sit, drew up another one for himself, and gave me a bottle of Coca-Cola.

"You'll pardon me, Mister," he began, "for seeming suspicious but we have to be careful. In ordinary times we wouldn't have anything to worry about, but with the war there's been some talk of the Federal government looking into lynchings. It seems there's some sort of law during wartime making it treason to lower the man power of the country."

"In that case I don't blame you for being careful," I assured him. "But couldn't the Federal government do something if it wanted to when a lynching takes place, even if no war is going on at the moment?"

"Naw," he said, confidently, obviously proud of the opportunity of displaying his store of information to one whom he assumed knew nothing whatever about the subject. "There's no such law, in spite of all the agitation by a lot of fools who don't know the niggers as we do. States' rights won't permit Congress to meddle in lynching in peace time."

"But what about your State government—your Governor, your sheriff, your police officers?"

"Humph! Them? We elected them to office, didn't we? And the niggers, we've got them disfranchised, ain't we? Sheriffs and police and Governors and prosecuting attorneys have got too much sense to mix in lynching-bees. If they do they know they might as well give up all idea of running for office any more—if something worse don't happen to them—" This last with a tightening of the lips and a hard look in the eyes.

I sought to lead the conversation into less dangerous channels. "Who was the white man who was killed—whose killing caused the lynchings?" I asked.

"Oh, he was a hard one, all right. Never paid his debts to white men or niggers and wasn't liked much around here. He was a mean 'un, all right, all right."

"Why, then, did you lynch the niggers for killing such a man?"

"It's a matter of safety—we gotta show niggers that they mustn't touch a white man, no matter how low-down and ornery he is."

Little by little he revealed the whole story. When he told of the manner in which the pregnant woman had been killed he chuckled and slapped his thigh and declared it to be "the best show, Mister, I ever did see. You ought to have heard the wench howl when we strung her up."

Covering the nausea the story caused me as best I could, I slowly gained the whole story, with the names of the other participants. Among them were prosperous farmers, business men, bankers, newspaper reporters and editors, and several law enforcement officers.

My several days of discreet inquiry began to arouse suspicions in the town. On the third day of my stay I went once more into the store of the man with whom I had first talked. He asked me to wait until he had finished serving the sole customer. When she had gone he came from behind the counter and with secretive manner and lowered voice he asked, "You're a government man, ain't you?" (An agent of the Federal Department of Justice was what he meant.)

"Who said so?" I countered.

"Never mind who told me; I know one when I see him," he replied, with a shrewd harshness in his face and voice.

Ignorant of what might have taken place since last I had talked with him, I thought it wise to learn all I could and say nothing which might commit me. "Don't you tell anyone I am a government man; if I *am* one, you're the only one in town who knows it," I told him cryptically. I knew that within an hour everybody in town would share his "information."

An hour or so later I went at nightfall to the little but not uncomfortable hotel where I was staying. As I was about to enter a Negro approached me and, with an air of great mystery, told me that he had just heard a group of white men discussing me and declaring that if I remained in the town overnight "something would happen" to me.

The thought raced through my mind before I replied that it was hardly likely that, following so terrible a series of lynchings, a Negro would voluntarily approach a supposedly white man whom he did not know and deliver such a message. He had been sent, and no doubt the persons who sent him were white and for some reason did not dare tackle me themselves. Had they dared there would have been no warning in advance—simply an attack. Though I had no weapon with me, it occurred to me that there was no reason why two should not play at the game of bluffing. I looked straight into my informant's eyes and said, in as convincing a tone as I could muster: "You go back to the ones who sent you and tell them this: that I have a damned good automatic and I know how to use it. If anybody attempts to molest me tonight or any other time, somebody is going to get hurt."

That night I did not take off my clothes nor did I sleep. Ordinarily in such small Southern towns everyone is snoring by nine o'clock. That night, however, there was much passing and re-passing of the hotel. I learned afterward that the merchant had, as I expected, told generally that I was an agent of the Department of Justice, and my empty threat had served to reinforce his assertion. The Negro had been sent to me in the hope that I might be frightened enough to leave before I had secured evidence against the members of the mob. I remained in the town two more days. My every movement was watched, but I was not molested. But when, later, it became known that not only was I not an agent of the Department of Justice but a Negro, the fury of the inhabitants of the region was unlimited—particularly when it was found that evidence I gathered had been placed in the hands of the Governor of Georgia. It happened that he was a man genuinely eager to stop lynching—but restrictive laws against which he had appealed in vain effectively prevented him from acting upon the evidence. And the Federal government declared itself unable to proceed against the lynchers.

III

In 1926 I went to a Southern State for a New York newspaper to inquire into the lynching of two colored boys and a colored woman. Shortly after reaching the town I learned that a certain lawyer knew something about the lynchers. He proved to be the only specimen I have ever encountered in much travelling in the South of the Southern gentleman so beloved by fiction writers of the older school. He had heard of the lynching before it occurred and, fruitlessly, had warned the judge and the prosecutor. He talked frankly about the affair and gave me the names of certain men who knew more about it than he did. Several of them lived in a small town nearby where the only industry was a large cotton mill. When I asked him if he would go with me to call on these people he peered out of the window at the descending sun and said, somewhat anxiously, I thought, "I will go with you if you will promise to get back to town before sundown."

I asked why there was need of such haste. "No one would harm a respectable and well-known person like yourself, would they?" I asked him.

"Those mill hands out there would harm anybody," he answered.

I promised him we would be back before sundown—a promise that was not hard to make, for if they would harm this man I could imagine what they would do to a stranger!

When we reached the little mill town we passed through it and, ascending a steep hill, our car stopped in front of a house perched perilously on the side of the hill. In the yard stood a man with iron gray hair and eyes which seemed strong enough to bore through concrete. The old lawyer introduced me and we were invited into the house. As it was a cold afternoon in late Autumn the gray-haired man called a boy to build a fire.

I told him frankly I was seeking information about the lynching. He said nothing but left the room. Perhaps two minutes later, hearing a sound at the door through which he had gone, I looked up and there stood a figure clad in the full regalia of the Ku Klux Klan. I looked at the figure and the figure looked at me. The hood was then removed and, as I suspected, it was the owner of the house.

"I show you this," he told me, "so you will know that what I tell you is true."

This man, I learned, had been the organizer and kleagle of the local Klan. He had been quite honest in his activities as a Kluxer, for corrupt officials and widespread criminal activities had caused him and other local men to believe that the only cure rested in a secret extra-legal organization. But he had not long been engaged in promoting the plan before he had the experience of other believers in Klan methods. The very people whose misdeeds the organization was designed to correct gained control of it. This man then resigned and ever since had been living in fear of his life. He took me into an adjoining room after removing his Klan robe and there showed me a considerable collection of revolvers, shot guns, rifles and ammunition.

We then sat down and I listened to as hair-raising a tale of Nordic moral endeavor as it has ever been my lot to hear. Among the choice bits were stories such as this: The sheriff of an adjoining county the year before had been a candidate for reëlection. A certain man of considerable wealth had contributed largely to his campaign fund, providing the margin by which he was reëlected. Shortly afterwards a married woman with whom the sheriff's supporter had been intimate quarreled one night with her husband. When the cuckold charged his wife with infidelity, the gentle creature waited until he was asleep, got a large butcher knife, and then artistically carved him up. Bleeding more profusely than a pig in the stock yards, the man dragged himself to the home of a neighbor several hundred yards distant and there died on the door-step. The facts were notorious, but the sheriff effectively blocked even interrogation of the widow!

I spent some days in the region and found that the three Negroes who had been lynched were about as guilty of the murder of which they were charged as I was. Convicted in a court thronged with armed Klansmen and sentenced to death, their case had been appealed to the State Supreme Court, which promptly reversed the conviction, remanded the appellants for new trials, and severely criticized the judge before whom they had been tried. At the new trial the evidence against one of the defendants so clearly showed his innocence that the judge granted a motion to dismiss, and the other two defendants were obviously as little guilty as he. But as soon as the motion to dismiss was granted the defendant was rearrested on a trivial charge and once again lodged in jail. That night the mob took the prisoners to the outskirts of the town, told them to run, and as they set out pumped bullets into their backs. The two boys died instantly. The woman was shot in several places, but was not immediately killed. One of the lynchers afterwards laughingly told me that "we had to waste fifty bullets on the wench before one of them stopped her howling."

Evidence in affidavit form indicated rather clearly that various law enforcement officials, including the sheriff, his deputies, various jailers and policemen, three relatives of the then Governor of the State, a member of the State Legislature and sundry individuals prominent in business, political and social life of the vicinity, were members of the mob.

The revelation of these findings after I had returned to New York did not add to my popularity in the lynching region. Public sentiment in the State itself, stirred up by several courageous newspapers, began to make it uncomfortable for the lynchers. When the sheriff found things getting a bit too unpleasant he announced that he was going to ask the grand jury to indict me for "bribery and passing for white." It developed that the person I was supposed to have paid money to for execution of an affidavit was a man I had never seen in the flesh, the affidavit having been secured by the reporter of a New York newspaper.

An amusing tale is connected with the charge of passing. Many years ago a bill was introduced in the Legislature of that State defining legally as a Negro any person who had one drop or more of Negro blood. Acrimonious debate in the lower house did not prevent passage of the measure, and the same result seemed likely in the State Senate. One of the Senators, a man destined eventually to go to the United States Senate on a campaign of vilification of the Negro, rose at a strategic point to speak on the bill. As the story goes, his climax was: "If you go on with this bill you will bathe every county in blood before nightfall. And, what's more, there won't be enough white people left in the State to pass it."

When the sheriff threatened me with an indictment for passing as white, a white man in the State with whom I had talked wrote me a long letter asking me if it were true that I had Negro blood. "You did not tell me nor anyone else in my presence," he wrote, "that you were white except as to your name. I had on amber-colored glasses and did not take the trouble to scrutinize your color, but I really did take you for a white man and, according to the laws of——, you may be." My information urged me to sit down and figure out mathematically the exact percentage of Negro blood that I possessed and, if it proved to be less than one-eighth, to sue for libel those who had charged me with passing.

This man wrote of the frantic efforts of the whites of his State to keep themselves thought of as white. He quoted an old law to the effect that "it was not slander to call one a Negro because everybody could see that he was not; but it was slanderous to call him a mulatto."

IV

On another occasion a serious race riot occurred in Tulsa, Okla., a bustling town of 100,000 inhabitants. In the early days Tulsa had been a lifeless and unimportant village of not more than five thousand people, and its Negro residents had been forced to live in what was considered the least desirable section of the village, down near the railroad. Then oil was discovered nearby and almost overnight the village grew into a prosperous town. The Negroes prospered along with the whites, and began to erect comfortable homes, business establishments, a hotel, two cinemas and other enterprises, all of these springing up in the section to which they had been relegated. This was, as I have said, down near the railroad tracks. The swift growth of the town made this hitherto disregarded land of great value for business purposes. Efforts to purchase the land from the Negro owners at prices far below its value were unavailing. Having built up the neighborhood and knowing its value, the owners refused to be victimized.

One afternoon in 1921 a Negro messenger boy went to deliver a package in an office building on the main street of Tulsa. His errand done, he rang the bell for the elevator in order that he might descend. The operator, a young white girl, on finding that she had been summoned by a Negro, opened the door of the car ungraciously. Two versions there are of what happened then. The boy declared that she started the car on its downward plunge when he was only halfway in, and that to save himself from being killed he had to throw himself into the car, stepping on the girl's foot in doing so. The girl, on the other hand, asserted that the boy attempted to rape her in the elevator. The latter story, at best, seemed highly dubious—that an attempted criminal assault would be made by any person in an open elevator of a crowded office building on the main street of a town of 100,000 inhabitants—and in open daylight!

Whatever the truth, the local press, with scant investigation, published lurid accounts of the alleged assault. That night a mob started to the jail to lynch the Negro boy. A group of Negroes offered their services to the jailer and sheriff in protecting the prisoner. The offer was declined, and when the Negroes started to leave the sheriff's office a clash occurred between them and the mob. Instantly the mob swung into action.

The Negroes, outnumbered, were forced back to their own neighborhood. Rapidly the news spread of the clash and the numbers of mobbers grew hourly. By daybreak of the following day the mob numbered around five thousand, and was armed with machine-guns, dynamite, rifles, revolvers and shotguns, cans of gasoline and kerosene, and—such are the blessings of invention!—airplanes. Surrounding the Negro section, it attacked, led by men who had been officers in the American army in France. Outnumbered and out-equipped, the plight of the Negroes was a hopeless one from the beginning. Driven further and further back, many of them were killed or wounded, among them an aged man and his wife, who were slain as they knelt at prayer for deliverance. Forty-four blocks of property were burned after homes and stores had been pillaged.

I arrived in Tulsa while the excitement was at its peak. Within a few hours I met a commercial photographer who had worked for five years on a New York newspaper and he welcomed me with open arms when he found that I represented a New York paper. From him I learned that special deputy sheriffs were being sworn in to guard the town from a rumoured counter attack by the Negroes. It occurred to me that I could get myself sworn in as one of these deputies.

It was even easier to do this than I had expected. That evening in the City Hall I had to answer only three questions—name, age, and address. I might have been a thug, a murderer, an escaped convict, a member of the mob itself which had laid waste a large area of the city—none of these mattered; my skin was apparently white, and that was enough. After we—some fifty or sixty of us—had been sworn in, solemnly declaring we would do our utmost to uphold the laws and constitutions of the United States and the State of Oklahoma, a villainous-looking man next me turned and remarked casually, even with a note of happiness in his voice: "Now you can go out and shoot any nigger you see and the law'll be behind you."

As we stood in the wide marble corridor of the not unimposing City Hall waiting to be assigned to automobiles which were to patrol the city during the night, I noticed a man, clad in the uniform of a captain of the United States Army, watching me closely. I imagined I saw in his very swarthy face (he was much darker than I, but was classed as a white man while I am deemed a Negro) mingled inquiry and hostility.

I kept my eye on him without appearing to do so. Tulsa would not have been a very healthy place for me that night had my race or my previous investigations of other race riots been known there. At last the man seemed certain he knew me and started toward me.

He drew me aside into a deserted corner on the excuse that he had something he wished to ask me, and I noticed that four other men with whom he had been talking detached themselves from the crowd and followed us.

Without further introduction or apology my dark-skinned newly-made acquaintance, putting his face close to mine and looking into my eyes with a steely, unfriendly glance, demanded challengingly:

"You say that your name is White?"

I answered affirmatively.

"You say you're a newspaper man?"

"Yes, I represent the New York—. Would you care to see my credentials?"

"No, but I want to tell you something. There's an organization in the South that doesn't love niggers. It has branches everywhere. You needn't ask me the name—I can't tell you. But it has come back into existence to fight this damned nigger Advancement Association. We watch every movement of the officers of this nigger society and we're out to get them for putting notions of equality into the heads of our niggers down South here."

There could be no question that he referred to the Ku Klux Klan on the one hand and the National Association for the Advancement of Colored People on the other. As coolly as I could, the circumstances being what they were, I took a cigarette from my case and lighted it, trying to keep my hand from betraying my nervousness. When he finished speaking I asked him:

"All this is very interesting, but what, if anything, has it to do with the story of the race riot here which I've come to get?"

For a full minute we looked straight into each other's eyes, his four companions meanwhile crowding close about us. At length his eyes fell. With a shrug of his shoulders and a half-apologetic smile, he replied as he turned away, "Oh, nothing except I wanted you to know what's back of the trouble here."

It is hardly necessary to add that all that night, assigned to the same car with this man and his four companions, I maintained a considerable vigilance. When the news stories I wrote about the riot (the boy accused of attempted assault was acquitted in the magistrate's court after nearly one million dollars of property and a number of lives had been destroyed) revealed my identity—that I was a Negro and an officer of the Advancement Society—more than a hundred anonymous letters threatening my life came to me. I was also threatened with a suit for criminal libel by a local paper, but nothing came of it after my willingness to defend it was indicated.

V

A narrower escape came during an investigation of an alleged plot by Negroes in Arkansas to "massacre" all the white people of the State. It later developed that the Negroes had simply organized a cooperative society to combat their economic exploitation by landlords, merchants, and bankers, many of whom openly practiced peonage. I went as a representative of a Chicago newspaper to get the facts. Going first to the capital of the State, Little Rock, I interviewed the Governor and other officials and then proceeded to the scene of the trouble, Phillips county, in the heart of the cotton-raising area close to the Mississippi.

As I stepped from the train at Elaine, the county seat, I was closely watched by a crowd of men. Within half an hour of my arrival I had been asked by two shopkeepers, a restaurant waiter, and a ticket agent why I had come to Elaine, what my business was, and what I thought of the recent riot. The tension relaxed somewhat when I implied I was in sympathy with the mob. Little by little suspicion was lessened and then, the people being eager to have a metropolitan newspaper give their side of the story, I was shown "evidence" that the story of the massacre plot was well-founded, and not very clever attempts were made to guide me away from the truth.

Suspicion was given new birth when I pressed my inquiries too insistently concerning the share-cropping and tenant-farming system, which works somewhat as follows: Negro farmers enter into agreements to till specified plots of land, they to receive usually half of the crop for their labor. Should they be too poor to buy food, seed, clothing and other supplies, they are supplied these commodities by their landlords at designated stores. When the crop is gathered the landowner takes it and sells it. By declaring that he has sold it at a figure far below the market price and by refusing to give itemized accounts of the supplies purchased during the year by the tenant, a landlord can (and in that region almost always does) so arrange it that the bill for supplies always exceeds the tenant's share of the crop. Individual Negroes who had protested against such thievery had been lynched. The new organization was simply a union to secure relief through the courts, which relief those who profited from the system meant to prevent. Thus the story of a "massacre" plot.

Suspicion of me took definite form when word was sent to Phillips county from Little Rock that it had been discovered that I was a Negro, though I knew nothing about the message at the time. I walked down West Cherry street, the main thoroughfare of Elaine, one day on my way to the jail, where I had an appointment with the sheriff, who was going to permit me to interview some of the Negro prisoners who were charged with being implicated in the alleged plot. A tall, heavy-set Negro passed me and, *sotto voce*,[2] told me as he passed that he had something important to tell me, and that I should turn to the right at the next corner and follow him. Some

[2] ***sotto voce***: Speaking in a low tone to avoid being overheard.

inner sense bade me obey. When we had got out of sight of other persons the Negro told me not to go to the jail, that there was great hostility in the town against me and that they planned harming me. In the man's manner there was something which made me certain he was telling the truth. Making my way to the railroad station, since my interview with the prisoners, (the sheriff and jailer being present,) was unlikely to add anything to my story, I was able to board one of the two trains a day out of Elaine. When I explained to the conductor—he looked at me so inquiringly—that I had no ticket because delays in Elaine had given me no time to purchase one, he exclaimed, "Why, Mister, you're leaving just when the fun is going to start! There's a damned yaller nigger down here passing for white and the boys are going to have some fun with him."

I asked him the nature of the fun.

"Wal, when they get through with him," he explained grimly, "he won't pass for white no more."

—1929

Marita Bonner 1898–1971

Born in Boston and educated at Radcliffe College, Marita Bonner was keenly aware of the privileges afforded by her education at an elite institution. As she observed in "On Being Young—a Woman—and Colored," her first publication, "All your life you have heard of the debt you owe 'Your People' because you have managed to have the things they have not largely had." Upon graduation from Radcliffe, Bonner taught high school in Virginia and in Washington, D. C. After marrying and settling in Chicago in 1930, Bonner continued to publish short stories throughout the 1930s, but published nothing between 1941 and her death in 1971.

Bonner's well-regarded contributions to *The Crisis* and *Opportunity* between 1925 and 1929 distinguish her as one of the most versatile writers associated with the New Negro Renaissance. Although she is best known for her 1925 essay "On Being Young—A Woman—and Colored," which won first place in the annual literary competition sponsored by *The Crisis* (presented here), and for her experimental play, "The Purple Flower" (1928), which has received the lion's share of recent scholarly attention, Bonner's forte was the short story. Most of Bonner's fifteen published stories portray with naturalistic detail the harsh realities of racism, sexism, and economic competition in urban environments.

"On Being Young—A Woman—and Colored" also shows that Bonner was an astute social critic. This essay takes readers on a journey from the naïve confidence of youth to the sober and disillusioned reality of adulthood. What turns Bonner bitter, specifically, is racial discrimination, the "Jim Crow" (segregationist) laws she experiences in the South, and the sameness of Ghetto life, where she finds people "milling around like live fish in a basket. Those at the bottom crushed into a sort of stupid apathy by the weight of those on top." This breeds anger: "You long to explode and hurt everything white; friendly; unfriendly." Bonner's essay quietly but effectively makes the point that racial discrimination harms both blacks and whites. Bonner also illustrates that prejudice must be ended before the bitterness destroys any hope for a future of racial growth and development, a future in which there is sympathy between whites and African Americans rather than a corrosive anger that eventually will explode.

Bonner's two essays, three plays, and twenty short stories (five previously unpublished) are collected in *Frye Street and Environs: The Collected Works of Marita Bonner* (1987).

Further Reading Allison Berg and Merideth Taylor, "Enacting Difference: Marita Bonner's *Purple Flower* and the Ambiguities of Race," *African American Review* 32.3 (1998): 469–480; Judith Musser, "African American Women and Education: Marita Bonner's Response to the 'Talented Tenth,'" *Studies in Short Fiction* 34.1 (1997): 73–85.

—Allison Berg, Michigan State University

On Being Young—a Woman—and Colored

You start out after you have gone from kindergarten to sheepskin[1] covered with sundry Latin phrases.

At least you know what you want life to give you. A career as fixed and as calmly brilliant as the North Star. The one real thing that money buys. Time. Time to do things. A house that can be as delectably out of order and as easily put in order as the doll-house of "playing-house" days. And of course, a husband you can look up to without looking down on yourself.

Somehow you feel like a kitten in a sunny catnip field that sees sleek, plump brown field mice and yellow baby chicks sitting coyly, side by side, under each leaf. A desire to dash three or four ways seizes you.

That's Youth.

But you know that things learned need testing—acid testing—to see if they are really after all, an interwoven part of you. All your life you have heard of the debt you owe "Your People" because you have managed to have the things they have not largely had.

[1] **sheepskin:** At the time, sheepskin was used to make parchment for diplomas.

So you find a spot where there are hordes of them—of course below the Line[2]—to be your catnip field while you close your eyes to mice and chickens alike.

If you have never lived among your own, you feel prodigal. Some warm untouched current flows through them—through you—and drags you out into the deep waters of a new sea of human foibles and mannerisms; of a peculiar psychology and prejudices. And one day you find yourself entangled—enmeshed—pinioned in the seaweed of a Black Ghetto.

Not a Ghetto, placid like the Strasse[3] that flows, outwardly unperturbed and calm in a stream of religious belief, but a peculiar group. Cut off, flung together, shoved aside in a bundle because of color and with no more in common.

Unless color is, after all, the real bond.

Milling around like live fish in a basket. Those at the bottom crushed into a sort of stupid apathy by the weight of those on top. Those on top leaping, leaping; leaping to scale the sides; to get out.

There are two "colored" movies, innumerable parties—and cards. Cards played so intensely that it fascinates and repulses at once.

Movies.

Movies worthy and worthless—but not even a low-caste spoken stage.

Parties, plentiful. Music and dancing and much that is wit and color and gaiety. But they are like the richest chocolate; stuffed costly chocolates that make the taste go stale if you have too many of them. That make plain whole bread taste like ashes.

There are all the earmarks of a group within a group. Cut off all around from ingress from or egress to other groups. A sameness of type. The smug self-satisfaction of an inner measurement; a measurement by standards known within a limited group and not those of an unlimited, seeing, world. ... Like the blind, blind mice. Mice whose eyes have been blinded.

Strange longing seizes hold of you. You wish yourself back where you can lay your dollar down and sit in a dollar seat to hear voices, strings, reeds that have lifted the World out, up, beyond things that have bodies and walls. Where you can marvel at new marbles and bronzes and flat colors that will make men forget that things exist in a flesh more often than in spirit. Where you can sink your body in a cushioned seat and sink your soul at the same time into a section of life set before you on the boards for a few hours.

You hear that up at New York this is to be seen; that, to be heard.

You decide the next train will take you there.

You decide the next second that that train will not take you, nor the next—nor the next for some time to come.

[2] **the Line:** The Mason-Dixon line is the boundary between Maryland and Pennsylvania, which was the northern limit of slave-owning U.S. states before the abolition of slavery.

[3] **Strasse:** Road (German).

For you know that—being a woman—you cannot twice a month or twice a year, for that matter, break away to see or hear anything in a city that is supposed to see and hear too much.

That's being a woman. A woman of any color.

You decide that something is wrong with a world that stifles and chokes; that cuts off and stunts; hedging in, pressing down on eyes, ears and throat. Somehow all wrong.

You wonder how it happens there that—say five hundred miles from the Bay State[4]—Anglo Saxon intelligence is so warped and stunted.

How judgment and discernment are bred out of the race. And what has become of discrimination? Discrimination of the right sort. Discrimination that the best minds have told you weighs shadows and nuances and spiritual differences before it catalogues. The kind they have taught you all of your life was best: that looks clearly past generalization and past appearance to dissect, to dig down to the real heart of matters. That casts aside rapid summary conclusions, drawn from primary inference, as Daniel[5] did the spiced meats.

Why can't they then perceive that there is a difference in the glance from a pair of eyes that look, mildly docile, at "white ladies" and those that, impersonally and perceptively—aware of distinctions—see only women who happen to be white?

Why do they see a colored woman only as a gross collection of desires, all uncontrolled, reaching out for their Apollos[6] and the Quasimodos[7] with avid indiscrimination?

Why unless you talk in staccato squawks—brittle as sea-shells—unless you "champ" gum—unless you cover two yards square when you laugh—unless your taste runs to violent colors—impossible perfumes and more impossible clothes—are you a feminine Caliban[8] craving to pass for Ariel?[9]

An empty imitation of an empty invitation. A mime; a sham; a copy-cat. A hollow re-echo. A froth, a foam. A fleck of the ashes of superficiality?

Everything you touch or taste now is like the flesh of an unripe persimmon.

...Do you need to be told what that is being...?

Old ideas, old fundamentals seem worm-eaten, out-grown, worthless, bitter; fit for the scrap-heap of Wisdom.

What you had thought tangible and practical has turned out to be a collection of "blue-flower" theories.

---

[4] **Bay State:** Massachusetts.

[5] **Daniel:** Reference to Daniel 1:8-19. Daniel refused to defile himself by eating the King of Babylon's spiced meat, but he still grew healthy and strong.

[6] **Apollo:** Sun-god of the Greeks and Romans, and patron of music and poetry. He was said to be extraordinarily attractive.

[7] **Quasimodo:** Reference to a physically deformed character in Victor Hugo's *The Hunchback of Notre Dame* (1831).

[8] **Caliban:** Servant in Shakespeare's *The Tempest*, who is described as malformed and ugly.

[9] **Ariel:** Enchanting spirit in *The Tempest.*

If they have not discovered how to use their accumulation of facts, they are useless to you in Their world.

Every part of you becomes bitter.

But—"In Heaven's name, do not grow bitter. Be bigger than they are"—exhort white friends who have never had to draw breath in a Jim-Crow train. Who have never had petty putrid insult dragged over them—drawing blood—like pebbled sand on your body where the skin is tenderest. On your body where the skin is thinnest and tenderest.

You long to explode and hurt everything white; friendly; unfriendly. But you know that you cannot live with a chip on your shoulder even if you can manage a smile around your eyes—without getting steely and brittle and losing the softness that makes you a woman.

For chips make you bend your body to balance them. And once you bend, you lose your poise, your balance, and the chip gets into you. The real you. You get hard.

...And many things in you can ossify...

And you know, being a woman, you have to go about it gently and quietly, to find out and to discover just what is wrong. Just what can be done.

You see clearly that they have acquired things.

Money; money. Money to build with, money to destroy. Money to swim in. Money to drown in. Money.

An ascendancy of wisdom. An incalculable hoard of wisdom in all fields, in all things collected from all quarters of humanity.

A stupendous mass of things.

Things.

So, too, the Greeks ... Things.

And the Romans. ...

And you wonder and wonder why they have not discovered how to handle deftly and skillfully, Wisdom, stored up for them—like the honey for the Gods on Olympus—since time unknown.

You wonder and you wonder until you wander out into Infinity, where—if it is to be found anywhere—Truth really exists.

The Greeks had possessions, culture. They were lost because they did not understand.

The Romans owned more than anyone else. Trampled under the heel of Vandals and Civilization, because they would not understand.

Greeks. Did not understand.

Romans. Would not understand.

"They." Will not understand.

So you find they have shut Wisdom up and have forgotten to find the key that will let her out. They have trapped, trammeled, lashed her to themselves with thews and thongs and theories. They have ransacked sea and earth and air to bring every treasure to her. But she sulks and will not work for a world with a whitish hue because it has snubbed her twin sister, Understanding.

You see clearly—off there is Infinity—Understanding. Standing alone, waiting for someone to really want her.

But she is so far out there is no way to snatch at her and really drag her in.

So—being a woman—you can wait.

You must sit quietly without a chip. Not sodden—and weighted as if your feet were cast in the iron of your soul. Not wasting strength in enervating gestures as if two hundred years of bonds and whips had really tricked you into nervous uncertainty.

But quiet; quiet. Like Buddha[10]—who brown like I am—sat entirely at ease, entirely sure of himself; motionless and knowing, a thousand years before the white man knew there was so very much difference between feet and hands.

Motionless on the outside. But on the inside?

Silent.

Still ... "Perhaps Buddha is a woman."

So you too. Still; quiet; with a smile, ever so slight, at the eyes so that Life will flow into and not by you. And you can gather, as it passes, the essences, the overtones, the tints, the shadows; draw understanding to yourself.

And then you can, when Time is ripe, swoop to your feet—at your full height—at a single gesture.

Ready to go where?

Why . . . Wherever God motions.

—1925

Langston Hughes 1902–1967

As discussed by Willie Harrell in Theme 14 of this series, Langston Hughes was one of the most significant writers and intellectuals of the New Negro Renaissance and American literature in the twentieth century. The three poems included here show his versatility as a social critic and activist. Consistently, Hughes illustrates that an African American will to resist atrocities exists, and that this will can itself in turn become militant and violent. Perhaps the most poignant of the three poems is "Song for a Dark Girl," which ironically incorporates the refrain of the "patriotic" song of

[10] **Buddha:** Title given by adherents of Buddhism to its founder, Śākyamuni, or Siddhārtha Gautama, who flourished in Northern India in the fifth century B.C.

the South—"Way Down South in the Land of Cotton"—to narrate a lynching that ends with a stark and moving image:

Way Down South in Dixie
    (Break the heart of me)
Love is a naked shadow
    On a gnarled and naked tree.

"Mulatto" presents more resistance to violence and oppression in its depiction of the rape of an African American woman by a white man who views her body as "a toy," but also the son's enduring insistence on being recognized as the white man's son, "a little yellow / Bastard boy." Finally, "Harlem" suggests that violence, racism, and suppression may eventually lead to a detonation. When a dream is deferred it may "dry up/ like a raisin in the sun." But it may also fester, crust, or develop into a cataclysmic rage. Hughes's implication is clear, and his poetry has a two-fold purpose: not only depicting the harm that racist violence does, but also warning white America that if steps are not taken to abate oppression, black anger finally will explode.

(For more on Hughes see Theme 14.)

Mulatto

I am your son, white man!

Georgia dusk
And the turpentine woods.
One of the pillars of the temple fell.

5 *You are my son!*
Like hell!

The moon over the turpentine woods.
The Southern night
Full of stars,
10 Great big yellow stars.
What's a body but a toy?
Juicy bodies
Of nigger wenches
Blue black
15 Against black fences.
O, you little bastard boy,
What's a body but a toy?
The scent of pine wood stings the soft night air.

What's the body of your mother?
20 Silver moonlight everywhere.
What's the body of your mother?
Sharp pine scent in the evening air.
A nigger night,
A nigger joy,
25 A little yellow
Bastard boy.

Naw, you ain't my brother.
Niggers ain't my brother.
Not ever.
30 *Niggers ain't my brother.*

The Southern night is full of stars,
Great big yellow stars.
O, sweet as earth,
Dusk dark bodies
35 Give sweet birth
To little yellow bastard boys.

Git on back there in the night,
You ain't white.
The bright stars scatter everywhere.
40 Pine wood scent in the evening air.
A nigger night,
A nigger joy.

I am your son, white man!

A little yellow
45 Bastard boy.

—1927

Song for a Dark Girl

Way Down South in Dixie
(Break the heart of me)
They hung my black young lover
To a cross roads tree.

5 Way Down South in Dixie
(Bruised body high in air)
I asked the white Lord Jesus
What was the use of prayer.

Way Down South in Dixie
10 (Break the heart of me)
Love is a naked shadow
On a gnarled and naked tree.

—1927

Harlem

What happens to a dream deferred?

Does it dry up
like a raisin in the sun?
Or fester like a sore—
5 And then run?
Does it stink like rotten meat?
Or crust and sugar over—
like a syrupy sweet?

Maybe it just sags
10 like a heavy load.

Or does it explode?

—1951

Sterling A. Brown 1901–1989

Hailed as the Dean of African American letters, Sterling Allen Brown devoted his poetry and prose to the redress of racist stereotypes and thus to the portrayal of black subjectivity and complexity—indeed, to black humanity. Poet, essayist, ethnographer, anthologist, teacher, and raconteur, Brown worked with his New Negro Renaissance cohorts to combine Western literary traditions and the black vernacular to create a new artistic vocabulary for the representation of African American folk culture.

Although Brown pursued most of his career at Howard University, he began by going south, immersing himself in African American folk culture. Brown toured the countryside meeting mythic figures such as Calvin "Big Boy" Davis, Mrs. Bibby, and Slim Greer, among others; he frequented churches, bars, juke joints, and parties, all a part of his intimate encounter with spirituals, work songs, hollers, ballads, and especially the blues. In a larger sense, he learned the patterns of speech, idioms, forms, and ethos defining African American folk culture. As a result, his poems in folk idiom reclaimed black vernacular for black artists. Previously, James Weldon Johnson had asserted that due to minstrelsy, black dialect could render only humor and pathos, but upon the publication of Brown's most successful volume, *Southern Road* (1932), Johnson effectively recanted and conceded Brown's artistic breakthrough.

Marked by an emphasis on performance and vocalization, Brown's poems tend to capture his personas in the perpetual process of self-recreation, most often in defiance of oppressive circumstances. The four poems presented here—mostly written in a non-vernacular voice—also indicate the enduring tension between oppression, violence, and black anger. They detail instances of oppression and specific political events—slavery and colonization (in "Strong Men"), economic and legal oppression (in "Bitter Fruit of the Bitter True"), prejudicial judicial systems as embodied by the imprisonment of the Scottsboro Boys (in "Song of Triumph"), and the failure to accurately record black history (in "Remembering Nat Turner"). Like Hughes, Brown meditates on the violence these oppressions might lead to, but also the enduring will and resistance of strong black men and women.

Further Reading Kimberly Benston, "Sterling Brown's After-Song: 'When de Saints Go Ma'ching Home' and the Performance of Afro-American Voice," *Callaloo* 5 (1982): 33–42; Joanne Gabbin, *Sterling A. Brown: Building the Black Aesthetic Tradition* (1985); Mark A. Sanders, *Afro-Modernist Aesthetics and the Poetry of Sterling A. Brown* (1999); John Edgar Tidwell, ed., "Oh, Didn't He Ramble: Sterling A. Brown (1901–1989)," *Black American Literature Forum*, 23.1 (1989): 89–112.

—Mark A. Sanders, Emory University

Strong Men

The young men keep coming on
The strong men keep coming on.
SANDBURG

They dragged you from homeland,
They chained you in coffles,[1]
They huddled you spoon-fashion[2] *in filthy hatches,*
They sold you to give a few gentlemen ease.

[1] **coffles:** A coffle was a line of slaves chained together.

[2] **spoon-fashion:** When being transported on ships, slaves were often placed below decks in the hold, one behind another, in positions that resembled stacked spoons.

5 *They broke you in like oxen,*
They scourged you,
They branded you,
They made your women breeders,
They swelled your numbers with bastards....
10 *They taught you the religion they disgraced.*

You sang:
Keep a-inchin' along
Lak a po' inch worm....

You sang:
15 *Bye and bye*
I'm gonna lay down dis heaby load....

You sang:
Walk togedder, chillen,
Dontcha git weary....
20 The strong men keep a-comin' on
The strong men git stronger.

They point with pride to the roads you built for them,
They ride in comfort over the rails you laid for them.
They put hammers in your hands
25 *And said—Drive so much before sundown.*[3]

You sang:
Ain't no hammah
In dis lan',
Strikes lak mine, bebby,
30 *Strikes lak mine.*

They cooped you in their kitchens,
They penned you in their factories,
They gave you the jobs that they were too good for,
They tried to guarantee happiness to themselves
35 *By shunting dirt and misery to you.*

You sang:
Me an' muh baby gonna shine, shine
Me an' muh baby gonna shine.
The strong men keep a-comin' on
40 The strong men git stronger....

[3] **Drive so much before sundown:** Here, the black men (most likely exploited workers) were commanded to drive railroad spikes and lay a certain amount of track.

They bought off some of your leaders
You stumbled, as blind men will . . .
They coaxed you, unwontedly soft-voiced. . . .
You followed a way.
45 *Then laughed as usual.*

They heard the laugh and wondered;
Uncomfortable,
Unadmitting a deeper terror . . . .
The strong men keep a-comin' on
50 Gittin' stronger . . . .

What, from the slums
Where they have hemmed you,
What, from the tiny huts
They could not keep from you—
55 *What reaches them*
Making them ill at ease, fearful?
Today they shout prohibition at you
"Thou shalt not this"
"Thou shalt not that"
60 *"Reserved for whites only"*
You laugh.

One thing they cannot prohibit—
The strong men . . . coming on
The strong men gittin' stronger.
65 Strong men. . . .
Stronger. . . .

—1931

Remembering Nat Turner[1]

(For R. C. L.)

We saw a bloody sunset over Courtland, once Jerusalem,[2]
As we followed the trail that old Nat took
When he came out of Cross Keys[3] down upon Jerusalem,
In his angry stab for freedom a hundred years ago.
5 The land was quiet, and the mist was rising,

[1] **Nat Turner** (1800–1831): Leader of a slave revolt on August 21, 1831 in which seventy-five slaves killed fifty-five whites. Turner was eventually caught, convicted, and executed on November 11, 1831.

[2] **Jerusalem:** County seat of Southampton County, Virginia. It was originally called Courtland.

[3] **Cross Keys:** Site of a Civil War battle.

Out of the woods and the Nottaway swamp,
Over Southampton the still night fell,
As we rode down to Cross Keys where the march began.

When we got to Cross Keys, they could tell us little of him,
10 The Negroes had only the faintest recollections:
"I ain't been here so long, I come from up roun' Newsome;
Yassah, a town a few miles up de road,
The old folks who coulda told you is all dead an' gone.
I heard something, sometime; I doan jis remember what.
15 'Pears lak I heard that name somewheres or other.
So he fought to be free. Well. You doan say."

An old white woman recalled exactly
How Nat crept down the steps, axe in his hand,
After murdering a woman and child in bed,
20 "Right in this here house at the head of these stairs"
(In a house built long after Nat was dead).
She pointed to a brick store where Nat was captured,
(Nat was taken in the swamp, three miles away)
With his men around him, shooting from the windows
25 (She was thinking of Harpers Ferry and old John Brown[4]).
She cackled as she told how they riddled Nat with bullets
(Nat was tried and hanged at Courtland, ten miles away).
She wanted to know why folks would comes miles
Just to ask about an old nigger fool.
30 "Ain't no slavery no more, things is going all right,
Pervided thar's a good goober market this year.
We had a sign post here with printing on it,
But it rotted in the hole, and thar it lays,
And the nigger tenants split the marker for kindling.
35 Things is all right, now, ain't no trouble with the niggers
Why they make this big to-do over Nat?"
As we drove from Cross Keys back to Courtland,
Along the way that Nat came down upon Jerusalem,
A watery moon was high in the cloud-filled heavens,
40 The same moon he dreaded a hundred years ago.
The tree they hanged Nat on is long gone to ashes,
The trees he dodged behind have rotted in the swamps.

The bus for Miami and the trucks boomed by,
And touring cars, their heavy tires snarling on the pavement.
45 Frogs piped in the marshes, and a hound bayed long,
And yellow lights glowed from the cabin windows.

[4] **John Brown** (1800–1859): White abolitionist who attacked the federal armory at Harper's Ferry, Virginia on October 16, 1859.

As we came back the way that Nat led his army,
Down from Cross Keys, down to Jerusalem,
We wondered if his troubled spirit still roamed the Nottaway,[5]
50 Or if it fled with the cock-crow at daylight,
Or lay at peace with the bones in Jerusalem,
Its restlessness stifled by Southampton clay.

We remembered the poster rotted through and falling,
The marker split for kindling a kitchen fire.

—1939

Song of Triumph

Let the band play Dixie.
And let the Rebel Yell resound.
Let daughters of the Confederacy
Be proud that once more virginal loveliness
5 Even in dingy courtrooms
Receives the homage of the poets.

Let us rush to Stone Mountain[1]
Uncover our heads, stand speechless before
Granite embodiments of our knighthood
10 Unfinished but everlasting,
"And truth and honor established here, forever."
Lo! Stonewall, preux chevalier,[2]
And Lee, majestic Arthur,[3] facing East.

Behind them, to the West
15 Scottsboro, Decatur.
Eight cowering Negroes in a jail[4]
Waiting for the justice
Chivalry as ever extends to them,
Still receiving the benefactions
20 Of *Noblesse Oblige.*[5]

---

[5] **Nottaway:** Tribe of Native Americans who still had a reservation in Southampton as late as 1825.

[1] **Stone Mountain:** Site near Atlanta, Georgia that was notorious in the 1920s because of rallies held by the Ku Klux Klan.

[2] **Stonewall . . . chevalier:** A reference to Thomas "Stonewall" Jackson (1824–1863), Confederate Civil War general who is described with a French term meaning "pure knight."

[3] **Lee . . . Arthur:** A comparison of Robert E. Lee (1807–1870), the Confederacy's most famous general, to King Arthur, suggesting another connection with chivalry.

[4] **Scottsboro . . . jail:** A reference to the case of the Scottsboro Boys, in which nine black youths were accused of raping two white women. The case strongly affected race relations in the United States.

[5] ***Noblesse Oblige:*** French for "nobility obligates." The idea here is that those with power or high status should be benevolent toward the less fortunate.

Oh, let us be proud.
Oh, let us, undefeated, raise again
The Rebel Yell.

—1980

Bitter Fruit of the Tree

They said to my grandmother: "Please do not be bitter,"
When they sold her first-born and let the second die,
When they drove her husband till he took to the swamplands,
And brought him home bloody and beaten at last.
5 They told her, "It is better you should not be bitter,
Some must work and suffer so that we, who must, can live,
Forgiving is noble, you must not be heathen bitter;
These are your orders: you *are* not to be bitter."
And they left her shack for their porticoed house.

10 They said to my father: "Please do not be bitter,"
When he ploughed and planted a crop not his,
When he weatherstripped a house that he could not enter,
And stored away a harvest he could not enjoy.
They answered his questions: "It does not concern you,
15 It is not for you to know, it is past your understanding.
All you need know is: you must not be bitter."

—1939, 1980

Kay Boyle 1903–1993

What kind of "communication" both conveys and amends racial injustice and atrocity? And what role can a white, middle-class writer have in confronting (without appropriating) the harm that racism does? These are some of the complex issues Kay Boyle raises in her "A Communication to Nancy Cunard," a poem written after the state of Alabama placed on trial, for the fourth time, some of the nine black men and boys (two of whom were thirteen) arrested in 1931 and falsely accused of gang-raping two white women on a train. As Ellen McWhorter argues, on one level Boyle's poem attempts to raise social and political awareness, while also acknowledging the limitations of poetry as an instrument of social activism. But on another level, as

McWhorter says, the poem also exhorts to action an audience empowered by "whiteness, maleness, universal 'wisdom,' and/or mastery of language."

Born in St. Paul, Minnesota, Boyle was the daughter of Howard Peterson Boyle, a lawyer, and Katherine Evans, a literary and social activist. Many of her poems, novels, short stories, and essays illustrate that art needs to engage with political issues. Boyle herself was also involved in political activism, working against the Vietnam war in 1966–1967 and for Amnesty International in her later years. Boyle's poem, then, may question whether art *is* politics, but her life and writing as a whole show that a strict separation between political and literary "communication" can never be maintained.

Further Reading Ellen McWhorter, "A Note on 'Communication to Nancy Cunnard,'" http://www.english.uiuc.edu/maps/poets/a_f/boyle/cunard.htm; Sandra Spanier, *Kay Boyle, Artist and Activist* (1986).

A Communication to Nancy Cunard[1]

These are not words set down for the rejected
Nor for outcasts cast by the mind's pity
Beyond the aid of lip or hand or from the speech
Of fires lighted in the wilderness by lost men
Reaching in fright and passion to each other.
This is not for the abandoned to hear.

It begins in the dark on a boxcar floor, the groaning
timber
Stretched from bolt to bolt above the freight-train wheels
That grind and cry aloud like hounds upon the trail, the
breathing weaving
Unseen within the dark from mouth to nostril, nostril to
speaking mouth.
This is the theme of it, stated by one girl in a boxcar
saying:
"Christ, what they pay you don't keep body and soul
together."
"Where was you working?" "Working in a mill town."
The other girl in the corner saying: "Working the men
when we could get them."
"Christ, what they pay you," wove the sound of breathing,
"don't keep shoes on your feet.
Don't feed you. That's why we're shoving on."

[1] Nancy Cunard (1896–1965): English writer and political activist who wrote on the case of the "Scottsboro Boys." All nine defendants were eventually paroled, freed, or pardoned, except for Haywood Patterson, who escaped prison and fled to Detroit, Michigan, where, after he was found by the FBI in 1950, the governor of the state prevented him from being extradited to Alabama for trial.

(This is not for Virginia Price or Ruby Bates,[2] the white girls dressed like boys to go; not for Ozie Powell, six years in a cell playing the little harp he played tap-dancing on the boxcar boards; not for Olen Montgomery, the blind boy traveling towards Memphis that night, hopping a ride to find a doctor who could cure his eyes; not for Eugene Williams or Charlie Weems, not for Willie Robertson nor for Leroy and Andy Wright, thirteen years old the time in March they took him off the train in Paint Rock, Alabama; this is not for Clarence Norris or Haywood Patterson,[3] sentenced three times to die.)

This is for the sheriff with a gold lodge pin
And for the jury venireman who said: "Now, mos'
folk don't go on
And think things out. The Bible never speaks
Of sexual intercourses. It jus' says a man knows a
woman.
So after Cain killed Abel he went off and knew a
woman
In the land of Nod. But the Bible tells as how
There couldn't be no human folk there then.
Now, jus' put two and two together. Cain had
offspring
In the land of Nod so he musta had him a female
baboon
Or chimpanzee or somethin' like it.
And that's how the nigger race begun."

This is for the Sunday-school teacher with the tobacco
plug
Who addressed the jury, the juice splattering on the wall,
Pleading: "Whether in overalls or furs a woman is
protected by the Alabama law
Against the vilest crime the human species knows. Now,
even dogs choose their mates,
But these nine boys are lower than the birds of the air,
Lower than the fish in the sea, lower than the beasts of the
fields.
There is a law reaching down from the mountaintops to
the swamps and caves—
It's the wisdom of the ages, there to protect the sacred
parts of the female species
Without them having to buckle around their middles
Six-shooters or some other method of defense."

[2] **Virginia Price . . . Ruby Bates:** *Victoria* Price and Ruby Bates are the women the "Scottsboro Boys" were accused of raping. Bates later recanted her testimony, although Price did not.

[3] **Ozie Powell . . . Haywood Patterson:** These are the names of the "Scottsboro Boys."

This is set down for the others: people who go
 and come,
Open a door and pass through it, walk in the
 streets
With the shops lit, loitering, lingering, gazing.
This is for two men riding, Deputy Sheriff
 Sandlin, Deputy Sheriff Blacock,
With Ozie Powell, handcuffed. Twelve miles out
 of Cullman
They shot him through the head.

THE TESTIMONY

Haywood Patterson:	*Victoria Price:*
"So here goes an I shell try Faitfully an I possibly can Reference to myself in particularly And concerning the other boys personal pride And life time upto now.	 "I cain't remember."
You must be patiene with me and remember Most of my English is not of much interest And that I am continually Stopping and searching for the word."	 "I cain't remember."

So here goes and I shall try faithfully as possible to tell you as I understand if not mistaken that Olen Montgomery, who was part blind then, kept saying because of the dark there was inside the boxcar and outside it: "It sure don't seem to me we're getting anywheres. It sure don't seem like it to me." I and my three comrades whom were with me, namely Roy Wright and his brother Andy and Eugene Williams, and about my character I have always been a good natural sort of boy, but as far as I am personally concerned about those pictures of me in the papers, why they are more or less undoubtedly not having the full likeness of me for I am a sight better-looking than those pictures make me out. Why all my life I spent in and around working for Jews in their stores and so on and I have quite a few Jew friends whom can and always have gave me a good reputation as having regards for those whom have regards for me. The depression ran me away from home, I was off on my way to try my very best to find some work some elsewhere but misfortune befalled me without a moving cause. For it is events and misfortune which happens to people and how some must whom are less fortunate have their lives taken from them and how people die in chair for what they do not do.

THE SPIRITUAL FOR NINE VOICES

I went last night to a turkey feast (Oh, God,
 don't fail your children now!)
My people were sitting there the way they'll sit in
 heaven
With their wings spread out and their hearts all
 singing
Their mouths full of food and the table set with
 glass
(Oh, God, don't fail your children now!)
There were poor men sitting with their fingers
 dripping honey
All the ugly sisters were fair. I saw my brother
 who never had a penny
With a silk shirt on and a pair of golden braces
And gems strewn through his hair.

(Were you looking, Father, when the sheriffs
 came in?
Was your face turned towards us when they had
 their say?)

 There was baked sweet potato and fried corn
  pone
 There was eating galore, there was plenty in
  the horn.
(Were you there when Victoria Price took the
 stand?
Did you see the state attorney with her drawers in
 his hand?
Did you hear him asking for me to burn?)

 There were oysters cooked in amplitude
 There was sauce in every mouth.
 There was ham done slow in spice and clove
 And chicken enough for the young and the
  old.

(Was it you stilled the waters on horse-swapping
 day
When the mob came to the jail? Was it you come
 out in a long tail coat
Come dancing high with the word in your
 mouth?)

I saw my sister who never had a cent
Come shaking and shuffling between the
seats.
Her hair was straight and her nails were
pointed
Her breasts were high and her legs double-
jointed.

(Oh, God, don't fail your children now!)

THE SENTENCE

Hear how it goes, the wheels of it traveling fast on the
rails
The boxcars, the gondolas running drunk through
the night.
Hear the long high wail as it flashes through stations
unlit
Past signals ungiven, running wild through a country
A time when sleepers rouse in their beds and listen
And cannot sleep again.
Hear it passing in no direction, to no destination
Carrying people caught in the boxcars, trapped on the
coupled chert cars
(Hear the rattle of gravel as it rides whistling through the
day and night.)
Not the old or the young on it, nor people with any
difference in their color or shape,
Not girls or men, Negroes or white, but people with this in
common:
People that no one had use for, had nothing to give to, no
place to offer
But the cars of a freight train careening through Paint
Rock, through Memphis,
Through town after town without halting.
The loose hands hang down, and swing with the
swing of the train in the darkness,
Holding nothing but poverty, syphilis white as a
handful of dust, taking nothing as baggage
But the sound of the harp Ozie Powell is playing
or the voice of Montgomery
Half-blind in oblivion saying: "It sure don't seem
to me like we're getting anywheres.
It don't seem to me like we're getting anywheres
at all."

—1937

Richard Wright 1908–1960

Violence, poverty, and racial oppression are strong forces in much of Wright's work, but he also seeks political alternatives to existing social conditions. Born Richard Nathaniel Wright on September 4, 1908, about twenty miles east of Natchez, Mississippi, he and his family moved through many impoverished and segregated areas. Wright's parents held multiple jobs until 1914, when they relocated to Memphis where Nathaniel, Richard's father, left the family for another woman. In 1917, Richard, his mother, and his brother lived with his uncle, Silas, an entrepreneur in Arkansas, but the family fled when white men, presumably jealous of his success, murdered Silas. (Wright's 1938 story "Long Black Song" features a character named Silas who also encounters racist violence.) No one was arrested for the crime, but it surely focused Wright's attention on racism and violence in the South, as did the later murder of the brother of a high school friend.

Wright saw education as a way to defeat poverty. He read works by H. L. Mencken, and from Mencken learned of Theodore Dreiser, Sinclair Lewis, Sherwood Anderson, and others whose work encouraged him to write and influenced his style. In 1929, Wright moved to a small apartment in Chicago, where he made enough money working as a postman to devote more time to writing.

Communist promises of economic and social equality also made an impact on him. Wright began crafting leftist poetry, and in 1934 he officially joined the communist party. Wright moved to New York in 1937 and wrote for the *Daily Worker* while also working for the Federal Writer's Project. His "Fire and Cloud" won first prize in a *Story* magazine contest that same year. In 1938, Wright published "Bright and Morning Star" in *The Masses*, a socialist journal, and this story reflects his interest in communism and its connection to race. With *Uncle Tom's Children* (1938), Wright received critical acclaim and enough encouragement to begin work on *Native Son* (1940), his novel based on the case of Robert Nixon, a young black man who was accused of murdering a white woman. The novel was a best-seller and received many favorable reviews.

Wright married Ellen Poplar, a communist organizer from Brooklyn in 1941, and their daughter, Julia, was born in 1942. This same year, Wright withdrew from the communist party after realizing that it did not offer the opportunities he sought. Wright soon published the autobiographical *Black Boy* (1945), which was also a best-seller and a critical success. He then moved to Paris with his family, and they became permanent expatriates. Over the next few years, he traveled through Africa and Spain. In 1960, Wright died of a heart attack. His posthumously published works include *Eight Men* (1961) and *Haiku: This Other World* (1998).

Although Wright is best known for *Native Son*, as "The Ethics of Living Jim Crow" and "Bright and Morning Star" demonstrate, his shorter pieces function as scathing social criticism for a society that well into the 1940s and 1950s attempted to keep African Americans segregated, illiterate, and demoralized. The harms perpetrated by whites against blacks are powerfully catalogued in these two works: brutality, castration, rape, and economic discrimination. This breeds a terror of whites in African Americans, but it also breeds a corrosive double-consciousness, as Wright says in "The Ethics of Living Jim Crow": "Here my Jim Crow education . . . was no longer brutally cruel, but subtly cruel. Here I learned to lie, to steal, to dissemble. I learned to play that dual role which every Negro must play if he wants to eat and live." Wright's goal in this piece, however, is not just to catalogue these wrongs, but in so doing to encourage change and growth. By taking his reader along the journey of the small boy who grows up scarred and traumatized by Jim Crow, by making his readers see the harm done through the boy's (and later the man's) own eyes, Wright impels his audience to move beyond the "ethics" of Jim Crow into a new kind of ethics that values and enfranchises all members of society, black and white.

Further Reading Kwame Anthony Appiah and Henry Louis Gates, Jr., eds., *Richard Wright: Critical Perspectives Past and Present* (1993); Michel Fabre, *The Unfinished Quest of Richard Wright* (1973); Keith Kinnamon and Michel Fabre, *Conversations with Richard Wright* (1993); Hazel Rowley, *Richard Wright: The Life and Times* (2001).

—Edward Dauterich, Kent State University

The Ethics of Living Jim Crow

An Autobiographical Sketch

I

My first lesson in how to live as a Negro came when I was quite small. We were living in Arkansas. Our house stood behind the railroad tracks. Its skimpy yard was paved with black cinders. Nothing green ever grew in that yard. The only touch of green we could see was far away, beyond the tracks, over where the white folks lived. But cinders were good enough for me and I never missed the green growing things. And anyhow cinders were fine weapons. You could always have a nice hot war with huge black cinders. All you had to do was crouch behind the brick pillars of a house with your hands full of gritty ammunition. And the first woolly black head you saw pop out from behind another row of pillars was your target. You tried your very best to knock it off. It was great fun.

I never fully realized the appalling disadvantages of a cinder environment till one day the gang to which I belonged found itself engaged in a war with the white boys who lived beyond the tracks. As usual we laid down our cinder barrage, thinking that this would wipe the white boys out. But they replied with a steady bombardment of broken bottles. We doubled our cinder barrage, but they hid behind trees, hedges, and the sloping embankments of their lawns. Having no such fortifications, we retreated to the brick pillars of our homes. During the retreat a broken milk bottle caught me behind the ear, opening a deep gash which bled profusely. The sight of blood pouring over my face completely demoralized our ranks. My fellow-combatants left me standing paralyzed in the center of the yard, and scurried for their homes. A kind neighbor saw me and rushed me to a doctor, who took three stitches in my neck.

I sat brooding on my front steps, nursing my wound and waiting for my mother to come from work. I felt that a grave injustice had been done me. It was all right to throw cinders. The greatest harm a cinder could do was leave a bruise. But broken bottles were dangerous; they left you cut, bleeding, and helpless.

When night fell, my mother came from the white folks' kitchen. I raced down the street to meet her. I could just feel in my bones that she would understand. I knew she would tell me exactly what to do next time. I grabbed her hand and babbled out the whole story. She examined my wound, then slapped me.

"How come yuh didn't hide?" she asked me. "How come yuh awways fightin'?"

I was outraged, and bawled. Between sobs I told her that I didn't have any trees or hedges to hide behind. There wasn't a thing I could have used as a trench. And you couldn't throw very far when you were hiding behind the brick pillars of a house. She grabbed a barrel stave, dragged me home, stripped me naked, and beat me till I had a fever of one hundred and two. She would smack my rump with the stave, and, while the skin was still smarting, impart to me gems of Jim Crow wisdom. I was never to throw cinders any more. I was never to fight any more wars. I was never, never, under any conditions, to fight *white* folks again. And they were absolutely right in clouting me with the broken milk bottle. Didn't I know she was working hard every day in the hot kitchens of the white folks to make money to take care of me? When was I ever going to learn to be a good boy? She couldn't be bothered with my fights. She finished by telling me that I ought to be thankful to God as long as I lived that they didn't kill me.

All that night I was delirious and could not sleep. Each time I closed my eyes I saw monstrous white faces suspended from the ceiling, leering at me.

From that time on, the charm of my cinder yard was gone. The green trees, the trimmed hedges, the cropped lawns grew very meaningful, became a symbol. Even today when I think of white folks, the hard, sharp outlines of white houses surrounded by trees, lawns, and hedges are present somewhere in the background of my mind. Through the years they grew into an overreaching symbol of fear.

It was a long time before I came in close contact with white folks again. We moved from Arkansas to Mississippi. Here we had the good fortune not to live behind the railroad tracks, or close to white neighborhoods. We lived in the very heart of the local Black Belt. There were black churches and black preachers; there were black schools and black teachers; black groceries and black clerks. In fact, everything was so solidly black that for a long time I did not even think of white folks, save in remote and vague terms. But this could not last forever. As one grows older one eats more. One's clothing costs more. When I finished grammar school I had to go to work. My mother could no longer feed and clothe me on her cooking job.

There is but one place where a black boy who knows no trade can get a job, and that's where the houses and faces are white, where the trees, lawns, and hedges are green. My first job was with an optical company in Jackson, Mississippi. The morning I applied I stood straight and neat before the boss, answering all his questions with sharp yessirs and nosirs. I was very careful to pronounce my *sirs* distinctly, in order that he might know that I was polite, that I knew where I was, and that I knew he was a *white* man. I wanted that job badly.

He looked me over as though he were examining a prize poodle. He questioned me closely about my schooling, being particularly insistent about how much mathematics I had had. He seemed very pleased when I told him I had had two years of algebra.

"Boy, how would you like to try to learn something around here?" he asked me.

"I'd like it fine, sir," I said, happy. I had visions of "working my way up." Even Negroes have those visions.

"All right," he said. "Come on."

I followed him to the small factory.

"Pease," he said to a white man of about thirty-five, "this is Richard. He's going to work for us."

Pease looked at me and nodded.

I was then taken to a white boy of about seventeen.

"Morrie, this is Richard, who's going to work for us."

"Whut yuh sayin' there, boy!" Morrie boomed at me.

"Fine!" I answered.

The boss instructed these two to help me, teach me, give me jobs to do, and let me learn what I could in my spare time.

My wages were five dollars a week.

I worked hard, trying to please. For the first month I got along O.K. Both Pease and Morrie seemed to like me. But one thing was missing. And I kept thinking about it. I was not learning anything and nobody was volunteering to help me. Thinking they had forgotten that I was to learn something about the mechanics of grinding lenses, I asked Morrie one day to tell me about the work. He grew red.

"Whut yuh tryin' t' do, nigger, get smart?" he asked.

"Naw; I ain' tryin' t' git smart," I said.

"Well, don't, if yuh know whut's good for yuh!"

I was puzzled. Maybe he just doesn't want to help me, I thought. I went to Pease.

"Say, are yuh crazy, you black bastard?" Pease asked me, his gray eyes growing hard.

I spoke out, reminding him that the boss had said I was to be given a chance to learn something.

"Nigger, you think you're *white*, don't you?"

"Naw, sir!"

"Well, you're acting mighty like it!"

"But, Mr. Pease, the boss said…"

Pease shook his fist in my face.

"This is a *white* man's work around here, and you better watch yourself!"

From then on they changed toward me. They said good-morning no more. When I was just a bit slow in performing some duty, I was called a lazy black son-of-a-bitch.

Once I thought of reporting all this to the boss. But the mere idea of what would happen to me if Pease and Morrie should learn that I had "snitched" stopped me. And after all the boss was a white man, too. What was the use?

The climax came at noon one summer day. Pease called me to his work-bench. To get to him I had to go between two narrow benches and stand with my back against a wall.

"Yes, sir," I said.

"Richard, I want to ask you something," Pease began pleasantly, not looking up from his work.

"Yes, sir," I said again.

Morrie came over, blocking the narrow passage between the benches. He folded his arms, staring at me solemnly.

I looked from one to the other, sensing that something was coming.

"Yes, sir," I said for the third time.

Pease looked up and spoke very slowly.

"Richard, *Mr.* Morrie here tells me you called me *Pease*."

I stiffened. A void seemed to open up in me. I knew this was the show-down.

He meant that I had failed to call him Mr. Pease. I looked at Morrie. He was gripping a steel bar in his hands. I opened my mouth to speak, to protest, to assure Pease that I had never called him simply *Pease*, and that I had never had any intentions of doing so, when Morrie grabbed me by the collar, ramming my head against the wall.

"Now, be careful, nigger!" snarled Morrie, baring his teeth. "*I* heard yuh call 'im *Pease!* 'N' if yuh say yuh didn't, yuh're callin' me a *lie*, see?" He waved the steel bar threateningly.

If I had said: No, sir, Mr. Pease, I never called you *Pease,* I would have been automatically calling Morrie a liar. And if I had said: Yes, sir, Mr. Pease, I called you *Pease*, I would have been pleading guilty to having uttered the worst insult that a Negro can utter to a southern white man. I stood hesitating, trying to frame a neutral reply.

"Richard, I asked you a question!" said Pease. Anger was creeping into his voice.

"I don't remember calling you *Pease*, Mr. Pease," I said cautiously. "And if I did, I sure didn't mean..."

"You black son-of-a-bitch! You called me *Pease*, then!" he spat, slapping me till I bent sideways over a bench. Morrie was on top of me, demanding:

"Didn't yuh call 'im *Pease?* If yuh say yuh didn't, I'll rip yo' gut string loose with this bar, yuh black granny dodger! Yuh can't call a white man a lie 'n' git erway with it, you black son-of-a-bitch!"

I wilted. I begged them not to bother me. I knew what they wanted. They wanted me to leave.

"I'll leave," I promised. "I'll leave right *now*."

They gave me a minute to get out of the factory. I was warned not to show up again, or tell the boss.

I went.

When I told the folks at home what had happened, they called me a fool. They told me that I must never again attempt to exceed my boundaries. When you are working for white folks, they said, you got to "stay in your place" if you want to keep working.

II

My Jim Crow education continued on my next job, which was portering in a clothing store. One morning, while polishing brass out front, the boss and his twenty-year-old son got out of their car and half dragged and half kicked a Negro woman into the store. A policeman standing at the corner looked on, twirling his nightstick. I watched out of the corner of my eye, never slackening the strokes of my chamois upon the brass. After a few minutes, I heard shrill screams coming from the rear of the store. Later the woman stumbled out, bleeding, crying, and holding her stomach. When she reached the end of the block, the policeman grabbed her and accused her of being drunk. Silently, I watched him throw her into a patrol wagon.

When I went to the rear of the store, the boss and his son were washing their hands at the sink. They were chuckling. The floor was bloody and strewn with wisps of hair and clothing. No doubt I must have appeared pretty shocked, for the boss slapped me reassuringly on the back.

"Boy, that's what we do to niggers when they don't want to pay their bills," he said, laughing.

His son looked at me and grinned.

"Here, have a cigarette," he said.

Not knowing what to do, I took it. He lit his and held the match for me. This was a gesture of kindness, indicating that even if they had beaten the poor old woman, they would not beat me if I knew enough to keep my mouth shut.

"Yes, sir," I said, and asked no questions.

After they had gone, I sat on the edge of a packing box and stared at the bloody floor till the cigarette went out.

That day at noon, while eating in a hamburger joint, I told my fellow Negro porters what had happened. No one seemed surprised. One fellow, after swallowing a huge bite, turned to me and asked:

"Huh! Is tha' all they did t' her?"

"Yeah. Wasn't tha' enough?" I asked.

"Shucks! Man, she's a lucky bitch!" he said, burying his lips deep into a juicy hamburger. "Hell, it's a wonder they didn't lay her when they got through."

III

I was learning fast, but not quite fast enough. One day, while I was delivering packages in the suburbs, my bicycle tire was punctured. I walked along the hot, dusty road, sweating and leading my bicycle by the handle-bars.

A car slowed at my side.

"What's the matter, boy?" a white man called.

I told him my bicycle was broken and I was walking back to town.

"That's too bad," he said. "Hop on the running board."

He stopped the car. I clutched hard at my bicycle with one hand and clung to the side of the car with the other.

"All set?"

"Yes, sir," I answered. The car started.

It was full of young white men. They were drinking. I watched the flask pass from mouth to mouth.

"Wanna drink, boy?" one asked.

I laughed as the wind whipped my face. Instinctively obeying the freshly planted precepts of my mother. I said:

"Oh, no!"

The words were hardly out of my mouth before I felt something hard and cold smash me between the eyes. It was an empty whisky bottle. I saw stars, and fell backwards from the speeding car into the dust of the road, my feet becoming entangled in the steel spokes of my bicycle. The white men piled out and stood over me.

"Nigger, ain' yuh learned no better sense'n tha' yet?" asked the man who hit me. "Ain' yuh learned t' say *sir* t' a white man yet?"

Dazed, I pulled to my feet. My elbows and legs were bleeding. Fists doubled, the white man advanced, kicking my bicycle out of the way.

"Aw, leave the bastard alone. He's got enough," said one.

They stood looking at me. I rubbed my shins, trying to stop the flow of blood. No doubt they felt a sort of contemptuous pity, for one asked:

"Yuh wanna ride t' town now, nigger? Yuh reckon yuh know enough t' ride now?"

"I wanna walk," I said, simply.

Maybe it sounded funny. They laughed.

"Well, walk, yuh black son-of-a-bitch!"

When they left they comforted me with:

"Nigger, yuh sho better be damn glad it wuz us yuh talked t' tha' way. Yuh're a lucky bastard, 'cause if yuh'd said tha' t' somebody else, yuh might've been a dead nigger now."

IV

Negroes who have lived South know the dread of being caught alone upon the streets in white neighborhoods after the sun has set. In such a simple situation as this the plight of the Negro in America is graphically symbolized. While white strangers may be in these neighborhoods trying to get home, they can pass unmolested. But the color of a Negro's skin makes him easily recognizable, makes him suspect, converts him into a defenseless target.

Late one Saturday night I made some deliveries in a white neighborhood. I was pedaling my bicycle back to the store as fast as I could, when a police car, swerving toward me, jammed me into the curbing.

"Get down and put up your hands!" the policemen ordered.

I did. They climbed out of the car, guns drawn, faces set, and advanced slowly.

"Keep still!" they ordered.

I reached my hand higher. They searched my pockets and packages. They seemed dissatisfied when they could find nothing incriminating. Finally, one of them said:

"Boy, tell your boss not to send you out in white neighborhoods after sundown."

As usual, I said:

"Yes, sir."

V

My next job was a hall-boy in a hotel. Here my Jim Crow education broadened and deepened. When the bell-boys were busy, I was often called to assist them. As many of the rooms in the hotel were occupied by prostitutes, I was constantly called to carry them liquor and cigarettes. These women were nude most of the time. They did not bother about clothing, even for bell-boys. When you went into their rooms, you were supposed to take their nakedness for granted, as though it startled you no more than a blue vase or a red rug. Your presence awoke in them no sense of shame, for you were not regarded as human. If they were alone, you could steal sidelong glimpses at them. But if they were receiving men, not a flicker of your eyelids could show. I remember one incident vividly. A new woman, a huge, snowy-skinned blonde, took a room on my floor. I was sent to wait upon her. She was in bed with a thick-set man; both were nude and uncovered. She said she wanted some liquor and slid out of bed and waddled across the floor to get her money from a dresser drawer. I watched her.

"Nigger, what in hell you looking at?" the white man asked me, raising himself upon his elbows.

"Nothing," I answered, looking miles deep into the blank wall of the room.

"Keep your eyes where they belong, if you want to be healthy!" he said.

"Yes, sir."

VI

One of the bell-boys I knew in this hotel was keeping steady company with one of the Negro maids. Out of a clear sky the police descended upon his home and arrested him, accusing him of bastardy. The poor boy swore he had had no intimate relations with the girl. Nevertheless, they forced him to marry her. When the child arrived, it was found to be much lighter in complexion than either of the two supposedly legal parents. The white men around the hotel made a great joke of it. They spread the rumor that some white cow must have scared the poor girl while she was carrying the baby. If you were in their presence when this explanation was offered, you were supposed to laugh.

VII

One of the bell-boys was caught in bed with a white prostitute. He was castrated and run out of town. Immediately after this all the bell-boys and hall-boys were called together and warned. We were given to understand that the boy who had been castrated was a "mighty, mighty lucky bastard." We were impressed with the fact that next time the management of the hotel would not be responsible for the lives of "trouble-makin' niggers." We were silent.

VIII

One night, just as I was about to go home, I met one of the Negro maids. She lived in my direction, and we fell in to walk part of the way home together. As we passed the white night-watchman, he slapped the maid on her buttock. I turned around, amazed. The watchman looked at me with a long, hard, fixed-under stare. Suddenly he pulled his gun and asked:

"Nigger, don't yuh like it?"

I hesitated.

"I asked yuh don't yuh like it?" he asked again, stepping forward.

"Yes, sir," I mumbled.

"Talk like it, then!"

"Oh, yes, sir!" I said with as much heartiness as I could muster.

Outside, I walked ahead of the girl, ashamed to face her. She caught up with me and said:

"Don't be a fool! Yuh couldn't help it!"

This watchman boasted of having killed two Negroes in self-defense.

Yet, in spite of all this, the life of the hotel ran with an amazing smoothness. It would have been impossible for a stranger to detect anything. The maids, the hall-boys, and the bell-boys were all smiles. They had to be.

IX

I had learned my Jim Crow lessons so thoroughly that I kept the hotel job till I left Jackson for Memphis. It so happened that while in Memphis I applied for a job at a branch of the optical company. I was hired. And for some reason, as long as I worked there, they never brought my past against me.

Here my Jim Crow education assumed quite a different form. It was no longer brutally cruel, but subtly cruel. Here I learned to lie, to steal, to dissemble. I learned to play that dual role which every Negro must play if he wants to eat and live.

For example, it was almost impossible to get a book to read. It was assumed that after a Negro had imbibed what scanty schooling the state furnished he had no further need for books. I was always borrowing books from men on the job. One day I mustered enough courage to ask one of the men to let me get books from the library in his name. Surprisingly, he consented. I cannot help but think that he consented because he was a Roman Catholic and felt a vague sympathy for Negroes, being himself an object of hatred. Armed with a library card, I obtained books in the following manner: I would write a note to the librarian, saying: "Please let this nigger boy have the following books." I would then sign it with the white man's name.

When I went to the library, I would stand at the desk, hat in hand, looking as unbookish as possible. When I received the books desired I would take them home. If the books listed in the note happened to be out, I would sneak into the lobby and forge a new one. I never took any chances guessing with the white librarian about what the fictitious white man would want to read. No doubt if any of the white patrons had suspected that some of the volumes they enjoyed had been in the home of a Negro, they would not have tolerated it for an instant.

The factory force of the optical company in Memphis was much larger than that in Jackson, and more urbanized. At least they liked to talk, and would engage the Negro help in conversation whenever possible. By this means I found that many subjects were taboo from the white man's point of view. Among the topics they did not like to discuss with Negroes were the following: American white women; the Ku Klux Klan; France, and how Negro soldiers fared while there; French women; Jack Johnson;[1] the entire northern part of the United States; the Civil War; Abraham Lincoln; U. S. Grant; General Sherman;[2] Catholics; the Pope; Jews; the Republican Party; slavery; social equality;

[1] **Jack Johnson:** John Arthur Johnson (1878–1946) was the first black Heavyweight Champion of the World in boxing from1908 to 1915.

[2] **General Sherman:** William Tecumseh Sherman (1820–1891) served in the United States Army during the Civil War and was known for his particularly brutal treatment of the South.

Communism; Socialism; the 13th and 14th Amendments[3] to the Constitution; or any topic calling for positive knowledge or manly self-assertion on the part of the Negro. The most accepted topics were sex and religion.

There were many times when I had to exercise a great deal of ingenuity to keep out of trouble. It is a southern custom that all men must take off their hats when they enter an elevator. And especially did this apply to us blacks with rigid force. One day I stepped into an elevator with my arms full of packages. I was forced to ride with my hat on. Two white men stared at me coldly. Then one of them very kindly lifted my hat and placed it upon my armful of packages. Now the most accepted response for a Negro to make under such circumstances is to look at the white man out of the corner of his eye and grin. To have said: "Thank you!" would have made the white man *think* that you *thought* you were receiving from him a personal service. For such an act I have seen Negroes take a blow in the mouth. Finding the first alternative distasteful, and the second dangerous, I hit upon an acceptable course of action which fell safely between these two poles. I immediately—no sooner than my hat was lifted—pretended that my packages were about to spill, and appeared deeply distressed with keeping them in my arms. In this fashion I evaded having to acknowledge his service, and, in spite of adverse circumstances, salvaged a slender shred of personal pride.

How do Negroes feel about the way they have to live? How do they discuss it when alone among themselves? I think this question can be answered in a single sentence. A friend of mine who ran an elevator once told me:

"Lawd, man! Ef it wuzn't fer them polices 'n' them ol' lynch-mobs, there wouldn't be nothin' but uproar down here!"

—1937

Bright and Morning Star

She stood with her black face some six inches from the moist windowpane and wondered when on earth would it ever stop raining. It might keep up like this all week, she thought. She heard rain droning upon the roof and high up in the wet sky her eyes followed the silent rush of a bright shaft of yellow that swung from the airplane beacon in far off Memphis. Momently she could see it cutting through the rainy dark; it would hover a second like a gleaming sword above her head, then vanish. She sighed, troubling, Johnny-Boys been trampin in this slop all day wid no decent shoes on his feet.... Through the window she could see the rich black earth sprawling outside in the night. There was more rain than the clay could soak up; pools stood

[3] **13th and 14th Amendments:** The 13th amendment outlawed slavery in the United States, and the 14th amendment required states to provide equal protection and due process to all persons under their jurisdiction.

everywhere. She yawned and mumbled: "Rains good n bad. It kin make seeds bus up thu the ground, er it kin bog things down lika watah-soaked coffin." Her hands were folded loosely over her stomach and the hot air of the kitchen traced a filmy vein of sweat on her forehead. From the cook stove came the soft singing of burning wood and now and then a throaty bubble rose from a pot of simmering greens.

"Shucks, Johnny-Boy coulda let somebody else do all tha runnin in the rain. Theres others bettah fixed for it than he is. But, naw! Johnny-Boy ain the one t trust nobody t do nothin. Hes gotta do it *all* hissef…"

She glanced at a pile of damp clothes in a zinc tub. Waal, Ah bettah git t work. She turned, lifted a smoothing iron with a thick pad of cloth, touched a spit-wet finger to it with a quick, jerking motion: *smiiitz!* Yeah; its hot! Stooping, she took a blue work-shirt from the tub and shook it out. With a deft twist of her shoulders she caught the iron in her right hand; the fingers of her left hand took a piece of wax from a tin box and a frying sizzle came as she smeared the bottom. She was thinking of nothing now; her hands followed a life-long ritual of toil. Spreading a sleeve, she ran the hot iron to and fro until the wet cloth became stiff. She was deep in the midst of her work when a song rose up out of the far off day of her childhood and broke through half-parted lips:

Hes the Lily of the Valley, the Bright n
Mawnin Star
Hes the Fairest of Ten Thousan t ma soul…[1]

A gust of wind dashed rain against the window. Johnny-Boy oughta c mon home n eat his suppah. Aw, Lawd! Itd be fine ef Sug could eat wid us tonight! Itd be like ol times! Mabbe aftah all it wont be long fo he comes back. Tha lettah Ah got from im last week said *Don give up hope….* Yeah; we gotta live in hope. Then both of her sons, Sug and Johnny-Boy, would be back with her.

With an involuntary nervous gesture, she stopped and stood still, listening. But the only sound was the lulling fall of rain. Shucks, ain no usa me ackin this way, she thought. Ever time they gits ready to hol them meetings Ah gits jumpity. Ah been a lil scared ever since Sug went t jail. She heard the clock ticking and looked. Johnny-Boys a *hour* late! He sho must be havin a time doin all tha trampin, trampin thu the mud…. But her fear was a quiet one; it was more like an intense brooding than a fear; it was a sort of hugging of hated facts so closely that she could feel their grain, like letting cold water run over her hand from a faucet on a winter morning.

She ironed again, faster now, as if she felt the more she engaged her body in work the less she would think. But how could she forget Johnny-Boy out there on those wet fields rounding up white and black Communists for a meeting tomorrow? And that was just what Sug had been doing when the sheriff had caught him, beat

[1] **Hes the Lily . . . soul:** Lines from the traditional hymn, "Lily of the Valley."

him, and tried to make him tell who and where his comrades were. Po Sug! They sho musta beat the boy somethin awfull! But, thank Gawd, he didnt talk! He ain no weaklin, Sug ain! Hes been lion-hearted all his life long.

That had happened a year ago. And now each time those meetings came around the old terror surged back. While shoving the iron a cluster of toiling days returned; days of washing and ironing to feed Johnny-Boy and Sug so they could do party work; days of carrying a hundred pounds of white folks' clothes upon her head across fields sometimes wet and sometimes dry. But in those days a hundred pounds was nothing to carry carefully balanced upon her head while stepping by instinct over the corn and cotton rows. The only time it had seemed heavy was when she had heard of Sug's arrest. She had been coming home one morning with a bundle upon her head, her hands swinging idly by her sides, walking slowly with her eyes in front of her, when Bob, Johnny-Boy's pal, had called from across the fields and had come and told her that the sheriff had got Sug. That morning the bundle had become heavier than she could ever remember.

And with each passing week now, though she spoke of it to no one, things were becoming heavier. The tubs of water and the smoothing iron and the bundles of clothes were becoming harder to lift, with her back aching so; and her work was taking longer, all because Sug was gone and she didn't know just when Johnny-Boy would be taken too. To ease the ache of anxiety that was swelling her heart, she hummed, then sang softly:

He walks wid me. He talks wid me
He tells me Ahm His own….

Guiltily, she stopped and smiled. Looks like Ah jus cant seem t fergit them ol songs, no mattah how hard Ah tries…. She had learned them when she was a little girl living and working on a farm. Every Monday morning from the corn and cotton fields the slow strains had floated from her mother's lips, lonely and haunting; and later, as the years had filled with gall, she had learned their deep meaning. Long hours of scrubbing floors for a few cents a day had taught her who Jesus was, what a great boon it was to cling to Him, to be like Him and suffer without a mumbling word. She had poured the yearning of her life into the songs, feeling buoyed with a faith beyond this world. The figure of the Man nailed in agony to the Cross, His burial in a cold grave, His transfigured Resurrection, His being breath and clay, God and Man—all had focused her feelings upon an imagery which had swept her life into a wondrous vision.

But as she had grown older, a cold white mountain, the white folks and their laws, had swum into her vision and shattered her songs and their spell of peace. To her that white mountain was temptation, something to lure her from her Lord, a part of the world God had made in order that she might endure it and come through all the stronger, just as Christ had risen with greater glory from the tomb. The days crowded with trouble had enhanced her faith and she had grown to love hardship with a bitter pride; she had obeyed the laws of the white folks with a soft smile of secret knowing.

After her mother had been snatched up to heaven in a chariot of fire, the years had brought her a rough workingman and two black babies, Sug and Johnny-Boy, all three of whom she had wrapped in the charm and magic of her vision. Then she was tested by no less than God; her man died, a trial which she bore with the strength shed by the grace of her vision; finally even the memory of her man faded into the vision itself, leaving her with two black boys growing tall, slowly into manhood.

Then one day grief had come to her heart when Johnny-Boy and Sug had walked forth demanding their lives. She had sought to fill their eyes with her vision, but they would have none of it. And she had wept when they began to boast of the strength shed by a new and terrible vision.

But she had loved them, even as she loved them now; bleeding, her heart had followed them. She could have done no less, being an old woman in a strange world. And day by day her sons had ripped from her startled eyes her old vision, and image by image had given her a new one, different, but great and strong enough to fling her into the light of another grace. The wrongs and sufferings of black men had taken the place of Him nailed to the Cross; the meager beginnings of the party had become another Resurrection; and the hate of those who would destroy her new faith had quickened in her a hunger to feel how deeply her new strength went.

"Lawd, Johnny-Boy," she would sometimes say, "Ah jus wan them white folks t try t make me tell *who* is *in* the party n who *ain!* Ah jus wan em t try, Ahll show em somethin they never thought a black woman could have!"

But sometimes like tonight, while lost in the forgetfulness of work, the past and the present would become mixed in her; while toiling under a strange star for a new freedom the old songs would slip from her lips with their beguiling sweetness.

The iron was getting cold. She put more wood into the fire, stood again at the window and watched the yellow blade of light cut through the wet darkness. Johnny-Boy ain here yit ... Then, before she was aware of it, she was still, listening for sounds. Under the drone of rain she heard the slosh of feet in mud. Tha ain Johnny-Boy. She knew his long, heavy footsteps in a million. She heard feet come on the porch. Some woman.... She heard bare knuckles knock three times, then once. Thas some of them comrades! She unbarred the door, cracked it a few inches, and flinched from the cold rush of damp wind.

"Whos tha?"

"Its me!"

"Who?"

"Me, Reva!"

She flung the door open.

"Lawd, chile, c mon in!"

She stepped to one side and a thin, blond-haired white girl ran through the door; as she slid the bolt she heard the girl gasping and shaking her wet clothes. Somethings wrong! Reva wouldna walked a mil t mah house in all this slop fer nothin! That gals stuck onto Johnny-Boy. Ah wondah ef anythin happened t im?

"Git on inter the kitchen, Reva, where its warm."

"Lawd, Ah sho is wet!"

"How yuh reckon yuhd be, in all tha rain?"

"Johnny-Boy ain here *yit?*" asked Reva.

"Naw! N ain no usa yuh worryin bout im. Jus yuh git them shoes off! Yuh wanna ketch yo deatha col?" She stood looking absently. Yeah; its somethin about the party er Johnny-Boy thas gone wrong. Lawd, Ah wondah ef her pa knows how she feels bout Johnny-Boy? "Honey, yuh hadn't oughta come out in sloppy weather like this."

"Ah had t come, An Sue."

She led Reva to the kitchen.

"Git them shoes off n git close t the stove so yuhll git dry!"

"An Sue, Ah got somethin t tell yuh…"

The words made her hold her breath. Ah bet its somethin bout Johnny-Boy!

"Whut, honey?"

"The sheriff wuz by our house tonight. He come t see pa."

"Yeah?"

"He done got word from somewheres bout tha meetin tomorrow."

"Is it Johnny-Boy, Reva?"

"Aw, naw, An Sue! Ah ain hearda word bout im. Ain yuh seen im tonight?"

"He ain come home t eat yit."

"Where kin he be?"

"Lawd knows, chile."

"Somebodys gotta tell them comrades that meetings off," said Reva. "The sheriffs got men watchin our house. Ah had t slip out t git here widout em followin me."

"Reva?"

"Hunh?"

"Ahma ol woman n Ah wans yuh t tell me the truth."

"Whut, An Sue?"

"Yuh ain tryin t fool me, is yuh?"

"*Fool* yuh?"

"Bout Johnny-Boy?"

"Lawd, naw, An Sue!"

"Ef theres anythin wrong jus tell me, chile. Ah kin stan it."

She stood by the ironing board, her hands as usual folded loosely over her stomach, watching Reva pull off her water-clogged shoes. She was feeling that Johnny-Boy was already lost to her; she was feeling the pain that would come when she knew it for certain; and she was feeling that she would have to be brave and bear it. She was like a person caught in a swift current of water and knew where the water was sweeping her and did not want to go on but had to go on to the end.

"It ain nothin bout Johnny-Boy, An Sue," said Reva. "But we gotta do somethin er we'll all git inter trouble."

"How the sheriff know about tha meetin?"

"Thas whut pa wants t know."

"Somebody done turned Judas."

"Sho looks like it."

"Ah bet it wuz some of them new ones," she said.

"Its hard t tell," said Reva.

"Lissen, Reva, yuh oughta stay here n git dry, but yuh bettah git back n tell yo pa Johnny-Boy ain here n Ah don know when hes gonna show up. *Some*bodys gotta tell them comrades t stay erway from yo pas house."

She stood with her back to the window, looking at Reva's wide, blue eyes. Po critter! Gotta go back thu all tha slop! Though she felt sorry for Reva, not once did she think that it would not have to be done. Being a woman, Reva was not suspect; she would *have* to go. It was just as natural for Reva to go back through the cold rain as it was for her to iron night and day, or for Sug to be in jail. Right now, Johnny-Boy was out there on those dark fields trying to get home. Lawd, don let em git im tonight! In spite of herself her feelings became torn. She loved her son and, loving him, she loved what he was trying to do. Johnny-Boy was happiest when he was working for the party, and her love for him was for his happiness. She frowned, trying hard to fit something together in her feelings: for her to try to stop Johnny-Boy was to admit that all the toil of years meant nothing; and to let him go meant that sometime or other he would be caught, like Sug. In facing it this way she felt a little stunned, as though she had come suddenly upon a blank wall in the dark. But outside in the rain were people, white and black, whom she had known all her life. Those people depended upon Johnny-Boy, loved him and looked to him as a man and leader. Yeah; hes gotta keep on; he cant stop now.... She looked at Reva; she was crying and pulling her shoes back on with reluctant fingers.

"Whut yuh carryin on tha way fer, chile?"

"Yuh done los Sug, now yuh sendin Johnny-Boy..."

"Ah got t, honey."

She was glad she could say that. Reva believed in black folks and not for anything in the world would she falter before her. In Reva's trust and acceptance of her she had found her first feelings of humanity; Reva's love was her refuge from shame and degradation. If in the early days of her life the white mountain had driven her back from the earth, then in her last days Reva's love was drawing her toward it, like the beacon that swung through the night outside. She heard Reva sobbing.

"Hush, honey!"

"Mah brothers in jail too! Ma cries ever day..."

"Ah know, honey."

She helped Reva with her coat; her fingers felt the scant flesh of the girl's shoulders. She don git ernuff t eat, she thought. She slipped her arms around Reva's waist and held her close for a moment.

"Now, yuh stop that cryin."

"A-a-ah c-c-cant hep it...."

"Everythingll be awright; Johnny-Boyll be back."

"Yuh think so?"

"Sho, chile. Cos he will."

Neither of them spoke again until they stood in the doorway. Outside they could hear water washing through the ruts of the street.

"Be sho n send Johnny-Boy t tell the folks t stay erway from pas house," said Reva.

"Ahll tell im. Don yuh worry."

"Good-bye!"

"Good-bye!"

Leaning against the door jamb, she shook her head slowly and watched Reva vanish through the falling rain.

She was back at her board, ironing, when she heard feet sucking in the mud of the back yard; feet she knew from long years of listening were Johnny-Boy's. But tonight, with all the rain and fear, his coming was like a leaving, was almost more than she could bear. Tears welled to her eyes and she blinked them away. She felt that he was coming so that she could give him up; to see him now was to say good-bye. But it was a good-bye she knew she could never say; they were not that way toward each other. All day long they could sit in the same room and not speak; she was his mother and he was her son. Most of the time a nod or a grunt would carry all the meaning that she wanted to convey to him, or he to her. She did not even turn her head when she heard him come stomping into the kitchen. She heard him pull up a chair, sit, sigh, and draw off his muddy shoes; they fell to the floor with heavy thuds. Soon the kitchen was full of the scent of his drying socks and his burning pipe. Tha boys hongry! She paused and looked at him over her shoulder; he was puffing at his pipe with his head tilted back and his feet propped up on the edge of the stove; his eyelids drooped and his wet clothes steamed from the heat of the fire. Lawd, tha boy gits mo like his pa every day he lives, she mused, her lips breaking in a slow, faint smile. Hols tha pipe in his mouth just like his pa usta ho his. Wondah how they woulda got erlong ef his pa hada lived? They oughta liked each other, they so mucha like. She wished there could have been other children besides Sug, so Johnny-Boy would not have to be so much alone. A man needs a woman by his side.... She thought of Reva; she liked Reva; the brightest glow her heart had ever known was when she had learned that Reva loved

Johnny-Boy. But beyond Reva were cold white faces. Ef theys caught it means *death*.... She jerked around when she heard Johnny-Boy's pipe clatter to the floor. She saw him pick it up, smile sheepishly at her, and wag his head.

"Gawd, Ahm sleepy," he mumbled.

She got a pillow from her room and gave it to him.

"Here," she said.

"Hunh," he said, putting the pillow between his head and the back of the chair.

They were silent again. Yes, she would have to tell him to go back out into the cold rain and slop; maybe to get caught; maybe for the last time; she didn't know. But she would let him eat and get dry before telling him that the sheriff knew of the meeting to be held at Lem's tomorrow. And she would make him take a big dose of soda before he went out; soda always helped to stave off a cold. She looked at the clock. It was eleven. Theres time yit. Spreading a newspaper on the apron of the stove, she placed a heaping plate of greens upon it, a knife, a fork, a cup of coffee, a slab of cornbread, and a dish of peach cobbler.

"Yo suppahs ready," she said.

"Yeah," he said.

He did not move. She ironed again. Presently, she heard him eating. When she could no longer hear his knife tinkling against the edge of the plate, she knew he was through. It was almost twelve now. She would let him rest a little while longer before she told him. Till one er'clock, mabbe. Hes so tired.... She finished her ironing, put away the board, and stacked the clothes in her dresser drawer. She poured herself a cup of black coffee, drew up a chair, sat down and drank.

"Yuh almos dry," she said, not looking around.

"Yeah," he said, turning sharply to her.

The tone of voice in which she had spoken had let him know that more was coming. She drained her cup and waited a moment longer.

"Reva wuz here."

"Yeah?"

"She lef bout a hour ergo."

"Whut she say?"

"She said ol man Lem hada visit from the sheriff today."

"Bout the meetin?"

She saw him stare at the coals glowing red through the crevices of the stove and run his fingers nervously through his hair. She knew he was wondering how the sheriff had found out. In the silence he would ask a wordless question and in the silence she would answer wordlessly. Johnny-Boys too trustin, she thought. Hes trying t make the party big n hes takin in folks fastern he kin git t know em. You cant trust ever white man yuh meet....

"Yuh know, Johnny-Boy, yuh been takin in a lotta them white folks lately..."

"Aw, ma!"

"But, Johnny-Boy..."

"Please, dont talk t me bout tha now, ma."

"Yuh ain t ol t lissen n learn, son," she said.

"Ah know whut yuh gonna say, ma. N yuh wrong. Yuh cant judge folks just by how yuh feel bout em n by how long yuh done knowed em. Ef we start that we wouldnt have *no*body in the party. When folks pledge they word t be with us, then we gotta take em in. Wes too weak t be choosy."

He rose abruptly, rammed his hands into his pockets, and stood facing the window; she looked at his back in a long silence. She knew his faith; it was deep. He had always said that black men could not fight the rich bosses alone; a man could not fight with every hand against him. But he believes so hard hes blind, she thought. At odd times they had had these arguments before; always she would be pitting her feelings against the hard necessity of his thinking, and always she would lose. She shook her head. Po Johnny-Boy; he don know...

"But ain nona our folks tol, Johnny-Boy," she said.

"How yuh know?" he asked. His voice came low and with a tinge of anger. He still faced the window and now and then the yellow blade of light flicked across the sharp outline of his black face.

"Cause Ah know em," she said.

"*Any*body mighta tol," he said.

"It wuznt nona *our* folks," she said again.

She saw his hand sweep in a swift arc of disgust.

"*Our* folks! Ma, who in Gawds name is *our* folks?"

"The folks we wuz born n raised wid, son. The folks we *know!*"

"We cant make the party grow tha way, ma."

"It mighta been Booker," she said.

"Yuh don know."

"...er Blattberg..."

"Fer Chrissakes!"

"...er any of the fo-five others whut joined las week."

"Ma, yuh jus don wan me t go out tonight," he said.

"Yo ol ma wans yuh t be careful, son."

"Ma, when yuh start doubtin folks in the party, then there ain no end."

"Son, Ah knows ever black man n woman in this parta the county," she said, standing too. "Ah watched em grow up; Ah even heped birth n nurse some of em; Ah knows em *all* from way back. There ain none of em that *coulda* tol! The folks Ah know jus don open they dos n ast death t walk in! Son, it wuz some of them *white* folks! Yuh just mark mah word n wait n see!"

"Why is it gotta be *white* folks?" he asked. "Ef they tol, then theys jus Judases, thas all."

"Son, look at whuts befo yuh."

He shook his head and sighed.

"Ma, Ah done tol yuh a hundred times. Ah cant see white n Ah cant see black," he said. "Ah sees rich men n Ah sees po men."

She picked up his dirty dishes and piled them in a pan. Out of the corners of her eyes she saw him sit and pull on his wet shoes. Hes goin! When she put the last dish away he was standing fully dressed, warming his hands over the stove. Jus a few mo minutes now n hell be gone, like Sug, mabbe. Her throat tightened. This black mans fight takes *ever*thin! Looks like Gawd put us in this world jus t beat us down!

"Keep this, ma," he said.

She saw a crumpled wad of money in his outstretched fingers.

"Naw, yuh keep it. Yuh might need it."

"It ain mine, ma. It berlongs t the party."

"But, Johnny-Boy, yuh might hafta go erway!"

"Ah kin make out."

"Don fergit yosef too much, son."

"Ef Ah don come back theyll need it."

He was looking at her face and she was looking at the money.

"Yuh keep tha," she said slowly. "Ahll give em the money."

"From where?"

"Ah got some."

"Where yuh git it from?"

She sighed.

"Ah been savin a dollah a week fer Sug ever since hes been in jail."

"Lawd, ma!"

She saw the look of puzzled love and wonder in his eyes. Clumsily, he put the money back into his pocket.

"Ahm gone," he said.

"Here; drink this glass of soda watah."

She watched him drink, then put the glass away.

"Waal," he said.

"Take the stuff outta yo pockets!"

She lifted the lid of the stove and he dumped all the papers from his pocket into the fire. She followed him to the door and made him turn round.

"Lawd, yuh tryin to maka revolution n yuh cant even keep yo coat buttoned." Her nimble fingers fastened his collar high around his throat. "There!"

He pulled the brim of his hat low over his eyes. She opened the door and with the suddenness of the cold gust of wind that struck her face, he was gone. She watched the black fields and the rain take him, her eyes burning. When the last faint footstep could no longer be heard, she closed the door, went to her bed, lay down, and pulled the cover over her while fully dressed. Her feelings coursed with the rhythm of the rain: Hes gone! Lawd, Ah *knows* hes gone! Her blood felt cold.

She was floating in a grey void somewhere between sleeping and dreaming and then suddenly she was wide awake, hearing and feeling in the same instant the thunder of the door crashing in and a cold wind filling the room. It was pitch black and she stared, resting on her elbows, her mouth open, not breathing, her ears full of the sound of tramping feet and booming voices. She knew at once: They lookin fer im! Then, filled with her will, she was on her feet, rigid, waiting, listening.

"The lamps burnin!"

"Yuh see her?"

"Naw!"

"Look in the kitchen!"

"Gee, this place smells like niggers!"

"Say, somebodys here er been here!"

"Yeah; theres fire in the stove!"

"Mabbe hes been here n gone?"

"Boy, look at these jars of jam!"

"Niggers make good jam!"

"Git some bread!"

"Heres some cornbread!"

"Say, lemme git some!"

"Take it easy! Theres plenty here!"

"Ahma take some of this stuff home!"

"Look, heres a pota greens!"

"N some hot cawffee!"

"Say, yuh guys! C mon! Cut it out! We didn't come here fer a feas!"

She walked slowly down the hall. They lookin fer im, but they ain got im yit! She stopped in the doorway, her gnarled, black hands as always folded over her stomach, but tight now, so tightly the veins bulged. The kitchen was crowded with white men in glistening raincoats. Though the lamp burned, their flashlights still glowed in red fists. Across her floor she saw the muddy tracks of their boots.

"Yuh white folks git outta mah house!"

There was a quick silence; every face turned toward her. She saw a sudden movement, but did not know what it meant until something hot and wet slammed her squarely in the face. She gasped, but did not move. Calmly, she wiped the warm, greasy liquor of greens from her eyes with her left hand. One of the white men had thrown a handful of greens out of the pot at her.

"How they taste, ol bitch?"

"Ah ast yuh t git outta mah house!"

She saw the sheriff detach himself from the crowd and walk toward her.

"Now, Anty..."

"White man, don yuh *Anty* me!"

"Yuh ain got the right sperit!"

"Sperit hell! Yuh git these men outta mah house!"

"Yuh ack like yuh don like it."

"Naw, Ah don like it, n yuh knows dam waal Ah don!"

"What yuh gonna do about it?"

"Ahm telling yuh t git outta mah house!"

"Gittin sassy?"

"Ef telling yuh t git outta mah house is sass, then Ahm sassy!"

Her words came in a tense whisper; but beyond, back of them, she was watching, thinking, judging the men.

"Listen, Anty," the sheriff's voice came soft and low. "Ahm here t hep yuh. How come yuh wanna ack this way?"

"Yuh ain never heped yo *own* sef since yuh been born," she flared. "How kin the likes of yuh hep me?"

One of the white men came forward and stood directly in front of her.

"Lissen, nigger woman, yuh talkin t *white* men!"

"Ah don care who Ahm talkin t!"

"Yuhll wish some day yuh did!"

"Not t the likes of yuh!"

"Yuh need somebody t teach yuh how t be a good nigger!"

"*Yuh* cant teach it t me!"

"Yuh gonna change yo tune."

"Not longs mah bloods warm!"

"Don git smart now!"

"Yuh git outta mah house!"

"Spose we don go?" the sheriff asked.

They were crowded around her. She had not moved since she had taken her place in the doorway. She was thinking only of Johnny-Boy as she stood there giving and taking words; and she knew that they, too, were thinking of Johnny-Boy. She knew they wanted him, and her heart was daring them to take him from her.

"Spose we don go?" the sheriff asked again.

"Twenty of yuh runnin over one ol woman! Now, ain yuh white men glad yuh so brave?"

The sheriff grabbed her arm.

"C mon, now! Yuh don did ernuff sass fer one night. Wheres tha nigger son of yos?"

"Don yuh wished yuh knowed?"

"Yuh wanna git slapped?"

"Ah ain never seen one of yo kind that wuznt too low fer..."

The sheriff slapped her straight across her face with his open palm. She fell back against a wall and sank to her knees.

"Is tha whut white men do t nigger women?"

She rose slowly and stood again, not even touching the place that ached from his blow, her hands folded over her stomach.

"Ah ain never seen one of yo kind tha wuznt too low fer..."

He slapped her again; she reeled backward several feet and fell on her side.

"Is tha whut we too low t do?"

She stood before him again, dry-eyed, as though she had not been struck. Her lips were numb and her chin was wet with blood.

"Aw, let her go! Its the nigger we wan!" said one.

"Wheres that nigger son of yos?" the sheriff asked.

"Find im," she said.

"By Gawd, ef we hafta find im well kill im!"

"He wont be the only nigger yuh ever killed," she said.

She was consumed with a bitter pride. There was nothing on this earth, she felt then, that they could not do to her but that she could take. She stood on a narrow plot of ground from which she would die before she was pushed. And then it was, while standing there feeling warm blood seeping down her throat, that she gave up Johnny-Boy, gave him up to the white folks. She gave him up because they had come tramping into her heart demanding him, thinking they could get him by beating her, thinking they could scare her into making her tell where he was. She gave him up because she wanted them to know that they could not get what they wanted by bluffing and killing.

"Wheres this meetin gonna be?" the sheriff asked.

"Don yuh wish yuh knowed?"

"Ain there gonna be a meetin?"

"How come yuh astin me?"

"There *is* gonna be a meetin," said the sheriff.

"Is it?"

"Ah gotta great mind t choke it outta yuh!"

"Yuh so smart," she said.

"We ain playing wid yuh!"

"Did Ah say yuh wuz?"

"Tha nigger son of yos is erroun here somewheres n Ah aim to find im," said the sheriff. "Ef yuh tell us where he is n ef he talks, mabbe hell git off easy. But ef we hafta find im, well kill im! Ef we hafta find im, then yuh git a sheet t put over im in the mawnin, see? Git yuh a sheet, cause hes gonna be dead!"

"He wont be the only nigger yuh ever killed," she said again.

The sheriff walked past her. The others followed. Yuh didnt git whut yuh wanted! she thought exultingly. N yuh ain gonna *never* git it! Hotly, something arched in her to make them feel the intensity of her pride and freedom; her heart groped to turn the bitter hours of her life into words of a kind that would make them feel that she had taken all they had done to her in stride and could still take more. Her faith surged so strongly in her she was all but blinded. She walked behind them to the door, knotting and twisting her fingers. She saw them step to the muddy ground. Each whirl of the yellow beacon revealed glimpses of slanting rain. Her lips moved, then she shouted:

"Yuh didnt git whut yuh wanted! N yuh ain gonna nevah git it!"

The sheriff stopped and turned; his voice came low and hard.

"Now, by Gawd, thas ernuff outta yuh!"

"Ah know when Ah done said ernuff!"

"Aw, naw, yuh don!" he said. "Yuh don know when yuh done said ernuff, but Ahma teach yuh ternight!"

He was up the steps and across the porch with one bound. She backed into the hall, her eyes full on his face.

"Tell me when yuh gonna stop talkin!" he said, swinging his fist.

The blow caught her high on the cheek; her eyes went blank; she fell flat on her face. She felt the hard heel of his wet shoes coming into her temple and stomach.

"Lemme hear yuh talk some mo!"

She wanted to, but could not; pain numbed and choked her. She lay still and somewhere out of the grey void of unconsciousness she heard someone say: *Aw fer chrissakes leave her erlone, its the nigger we wan....*

She never knew how long she had lain huddled in the dark hallway. Her first returning feeling was of a nameless fear crowding the inside of her, then a deep pain spreading from her temple downward over her body. Her ears were filled with the drone of rain and she shuddered from the cold wind blowing through the door. She opened her eyes and at first saw nothing. As if she were imagining it, she knew she was half lying and half sitting in a corner against a wall. With difficulty she twisted her neck and what she saw made her hold her breath—a vast white blur was suspended directly above her. For a moment she could not tell if her fear was from the blur or if the blur was from her fear. Gradually the blur resolved itself into a huge white face that slowly filled her vision. She was stone still, conscious really of the effort to breathe, feeling somehow that she existed only by the mercy of that white face. She had seen it before; its fear had gripped her many times; it had for her the fear of all the white faces she had ever seen in her life. *Sue* ... As from a great distance, she heard her name being called. She was regaining consciousness now, but the fear was coming with her. She looked into the face of a white man, wanting to scream out for him to go; yet accepting his presence because she felt she had to. Though some remote part of her mind was active, her limbs were powerless. It was as if an invisible knife had split her in two, leaving one half of her lying there helpless, while the other half shrank in dread from a forgotten but familiar enemy. *Sue its me Sue its me* ... Then all at once the voice came clearly.

"Sue, its me! Its Booker!"

And she heard an answering voice speaking inside of her. Yeah, its Booker ... The one whut just joined ... She roused herself, struggling for full consciousness; and as she did so she transferred to the person of Booker the nameless fear she felt. It seemed that Booker towered above her as a challenge to her right to exist upon the earth.

"Yuh awright?"

She did not answer; she started violently to her feet and fell.

"Sue, yuh hurt!"

"Yeah," she breathed.

"Where they hit yuh?"

"Its mah head," she whispered.

She was speaking even though she did not want to; the fear that had hold of her compelled her.

"They beat yuh?"

"Yeah."

"Them bastards! Them Gawddam bastards!"

She heard him saying it over and over; then she felt herself being lifted.

"Naw!" she gasped.

"Ahma take yuh t the kitchen!"

"Put me down!"

"But yuh cant stay here like this!"

She shrank in his arms and pushed her hands against his body; when she was in the kitchen she freed herself, sank into a chair, and held tightly to its back. She looked wonderingly at Booker. There was nothing about him that should frighten her so, but even that did not ease her tension. She saw him go to the water bucket, wet his handkerchief, wring it, and offer it to her. Distrustfully, she stared at the damp cloth.

"Here; put this on yo fohead ..."

"Naw!"

"C mon; itll make yuh feel bettah!"

She hesitated in confusion. What right had she to be afraid when someone was acting as kindly as this toward her? Reluctantly, she leaned forward and pressed the damp cloth to her head. It helped. With each passing minute she was catching hold of herself, yet wondering why she felt as she did.

"Whut happened?"

"Ah don know."

"Yuh feel bettah?"

"Yeah."

"Who all wuz here?"

"Ah don know," she said again.

"Yo head still hurt?"

"Yeah."

"Gee, Ahm sorry."

"Ahm awright," she sighed and buried her face in her hands.

She felt him touch her shoulder.

"Sue, Ah got some bad news fer yuh…"

She knew; she stiffened and grew cold. It had happened; she stared dry-eyed, with compressed lips.

"Its mah Johnny-Boy," she said.

"Yeah; Ahm awful sorry t hafta tell yuh this way. But Ah thought yuh oughta know…"

Her tension eased and a vacant place opened up inside of her. A voice whispered, Jesus, hep me!

"W-w-where is he?"

"They got im out t Foleys Woods tryin t make him tell who the others is."

"He ain gonna tell," she said. "They jus as waal kill im, cause he ain gonna nevah tell."

"Ah hope he don," said Booker. "But he didnt have a chance t tell the others. They grabbed im jus as he got t the woods."

Then all the horror of it flashed upon her; she saw flung out over the rainy countryside an array of shacks where white and black comrades were sleeping; in the morning they would be rising and going to Lem's; then they would be caught. And that meant terror, prison, and death. The comrades would have to be told; she would have to tell them; she could not entrust Johnny-Boy's work to another, and especially not to Booker as long as she felt toward him as she did. Gripping the bottom of the chair with both hands, she tried to rise; the room blurred and she swayed. She found herself resting in Booker's arms.

"Lemme go!"

"Sue, yuh too weak t walk!"

"Ah gotta tell em!" she said.

"Set down, Sue! Yuh hurt! Yuh sick!"

When seated, she looked at him helplessly.

"Sue, lissen! Johnny-Boys caught. Ahm here. Yuh tell me who they is n Ahll tell em."

She stared at the floor and did not answer. Yes; she was too weak to go. There was no way for her to tramp all those miles through the rain tonight. But should she tell

Booker? If only she had somebody like Reva to talk to! She did not want to decide alone; she must make no mistake about this. She felt Booker's fingers pressing on her arm and it was as though the white mountain was pushing her to the edge of a sheer height; she again exclaimed inwardly. Jesus, hep me! Booker's white face was at her side, waiting. Would she be doing right to tell him? Suppose she did not tell and then the comrades were caught? She could not ever forgive herself for doing a thing like that. But maybe she was wrong; maybe her fear was what Johnny-Boy had always called "jus foolishness." She remembered his saying, Ma, we cant make the party grow ef we start doubtin everbody....

"Tell me who they is, Sue, n Ahll tell em. Ah jus joined n Ah don know who they is."

"Ah don know who they is," she said.

"Yuh *gotta* tell me who they is, Sue!"

"Ah tol yuh Ah don know!"

"Yuh *do* know! C mon! Set up n talk!"

"Naw!"

"Yuh wan em all t git *killed?*"

She shook her head and swallowed. Lawd, Ah don believe in this man!

"Lissen, Ahll call the names n yuh tell me which ones is in the party n which ones ain, see?"

"Naw!"

"Please, Sue!"

"Ah don know," she said.

"Sue, yuh ain doin right by em. Johnny-Boy wouldnt wan yuh t be this way. Hes out there holdin up his end. Les hol up ours..."

"Lawd, Ah don know..."

"Is yuh scared a me cause Ahm *white?* Johnny-Boy ain like tha. Don let all the work we done go fer nothin."

She gave up and bowed her head in her hands.

"Is it Johnson? Tell me, Sue?"

"Yeah," she whispered in horror; a mounting horror of feeling herself being undone.

"Is it Green?"

"Yeah."

"Murphy?"

"Lawd, Ah don know!"

"Yuh gotta tell me, Sue!"

"Mistah Booker, please leave me erlone..."

"Is it Murphy?"

She answered yes to the names of Johnny-Boy's comrades; she answered until he asked her no more. Then she thought, How he know the sheriffs men is watchin

Lems house? She stood up and held onto her chair, feeling something sure and firm within her.

"How yuh know bout Lem?"

"Why … How Ah know?"

"Whut yuh doin here this tima night? How yuh know the sheriff got Johnny-Boy?"

"Sue, don yuh believe in me?"

She did not, but she could not answer. She stared at him until her lips hung open; she was searching deep within herself for certainty.

"You meet Reva?" she asked.

"Reva?"

"Yeah; Lems gal?"

"Oh, yeah. Sho, Ah met Reva."

"She tell yuh?"

She asked the question more of herself than of him; she longed to believe.

"Yeah," he said softly. "Ah reckon Ah oughta be goin t tell em now."

"Who?" she asked. "Tell *who?*"

The muscles of her body were stiff as she waited for his answer; she felt as though life depended upon it.

"The comrades," he said.

"Yeah," she sighed.

She did not know when he left; she was not looking or listening. She just suddenly saw the room empty and from her the thing that had made her fearful was gone.

For a space of time that seemed to her as long as she had been upon the earth, she sat huddled over the cold stove. One minute she would say to herself, They both gone now; Johnny-Boy n Sug … Mabbe Ahll never see em ergin. Then a surge of guilt would blot out her longing. "Lawd, Ah shouldna tol!" she mumbled. "But no man kin be so lowdown as to do a thing like that…" Several times she had an impulse to try to tell the comrades herself; she was feeling a little better now. But what good would that do? She had told Booker the names. He jus couldnt be a Judas to po folks like us … He *couldnt!*

"An Sue!"

Thas Reva! Her heart leaped with an anxious gladness. She rose without answering and limped down the dark hallway. Through the open door, against the background of rain, she saw Reva's face lit now and then to whiteness by the whirling beams of the beacon. She was about to call, but a thought checked her. Jesus, hep me! Ah gotta tell her bout Johnny-Boy … Lawd, Ah cant!

"An Sue, yuh there?"

"C mon in, chile!"

She caught Reva and held her close for a moment without speaking.

"Lawd, Ahm sho glad yuh here," she said at last.

"Ah thought somethin had happened t yuh," said Reva, pulling away. "Ah saw the do open … Pa told me to come back n stay wid yuh tonight…" Reva paused and started, "W-w-whuts the mattah?"

She was so full of having Reva with her that she did not understand what the question meant.

"Hunh?"

"Yo neck…"

"Aw, it ain nothin, chile. C mon in the kitchen."

"But theres blood on yo neck!"

"The sheriff wuz here…"

"Them fools! Whut they wanna bother yuh fer? Ah could kill em! So hep me Gawd, Ah could!"

"It ain nothin," she said.

She was wondering how to tell Reva about Johnny-Boy and Booker. Ahll wait a lil while longer, she thought. Now that Reva was here, her fear did not seem as awful as before.

"C mon, lemme fix yo head, An Sue. Yuh hurt."

They went to the kitchen. She sat silent while Reva dressed her scalp. She was feeling better now; in just a little while she would tell Reva. She felt the girl's finger pressing gently upon her head.

"Tha hurt?"

"A lil, chile."

"Yuh po thing."

"It ain nothin."

"Did Johnny-Boy come?"

She hesitated.

"Yeah."

"He done gone t tell the others?"

Reva's voice sounded so clear and confident that it mocked her. Lawd, Ah cant tell this chile…

"Yuh tol im, didnt yuh, An Sue?"

"Y-y-yeah…"

"Gee! Thas good! Ah tol pa he didnt hafta worry ef Johnny-Boy got the news. Mabbe thingsll come out awright."

"Ah hope…"

She could not go on; she had gone as far as she could. For the first time that night she began to cry.

"Hush, An Sue! Yuh awways been brave. Itll be awright!"

"Ain nothin awright, chile. The worls jus too much fer us, Ah reckon."

"Ef yuh cry that way itll make me cry."

She forced herself to stop. Naw; Ah cant carry on this way in fronta Reva ... Right now she had a deep need for Reva to believe in her. She watched the girl get pine-knots from behind the stove, rekindle the fire, and put on the coffee pot.

"Yuh wan some cawffee?" Reva asked.

"Naw, honey."

"Aw, c mon, An Sue."

"Jusa lil, honey."

"Thas the way to be. Oh, say, Ah fergot," said Reva, measuring out spoonsful of coffee. "Pa tol me t tell yuh t watch out fer tha Booker man. Hes a stool."

She showed not one sign of outward movement or expression, but as the words fell from Reva's lips she went limp inside.

"Pa tol me soon as Ah got back home. He got word from town..."

She stopped listening. She felt as though she had been slapped to the extreme outer edge of life, into a cold darkness. She knew now what she had felt when she had looked up out of her fog of pain and had seen Booker. It was the image of all the white folks, and the fear that went with them, that she had seen and felt during her lifetime. And again, for the second time that night, something she had felt had come true. All she could say to herself was, Ah didnt like im! Gawd knows, Ah didnt! Ah tol Johnny-Boy it wuz some of them white folks...

"Here; drink yo cawffee..."

She took the cup; her fingers trembled, and the steaming liquid spilt onto her dress and leg.

"Ahm sorry, An Sue!"

Her leg was scalded, but the pain did not bother her.

"Its awright," she said.

"Wait; lemme put some lard on tha burn!"

"It don hurt."

"Yuh worried bout somethin."

"Naw, honey."

"Lemme fix yuh so mo cawffee."

"Ah don wan nothin now, Reva."

"Waal, buck up. Don be tha way..."

They were silent. She heard Reva drinking. No; she would not tell Reva; Reva was all she had left. But she had to do something, some way, somehow. She was undone too much as it was; and to tell Reva about Booker or Johnny-Boy was more than she was equal to; it would be too coldly shameful. She wanted to be alone and fight this thing out with herself.

"Go t bed, honey. Yuh tired."

"Naw; Ahm awright, An Sue."

She heard the bottom of Reva's empty cup clank against the top of the stove. Ah *got* t make her go t bed! Yes; Booker would tell the names of the comrades to the sheriff. If she could only stop him some way! That was the answer, the point, the star that grew bright in the morning of new hope. Soon, maybe half an hour from now, Booker would reach Foleys Woods. Hes boun t go the long way, cause he don know no short cut, she thought. Ah could wade the creek n beat im there .... But what would she do after that?

"Reva, honey, go t bed. Ahm awright. Yuh need res."

"Ah ain sleepy, An Sue."

"Ah knows whuts bes fer yuh, chile. Yuh tired n wet."

"Ah wanna stay up wid yuh."

She forced a smile and said:

"Ah don think they gonna hurt Johnny-Boy..."

"Fer *real*, An Sue?"

"Sho, honey."

"But Ah wanna wait up wid yuh."

"Thas mah job, honey. Thas whut a mas fer, t wait up fer her chullun."

"Good night, An Sue."

"Good night, honey."

She watched Reva pull up and leave the kitchen; presently she heard the shucks in the mattress whispering, and she knew that Reva had gone to bed. She was alone. Through the cracks of the stove she saw the fire dying to grey ashes; the room was growing cold again. The yellow beacon continued to flit past the window and the rain still drummed. Yes; she was alone; she had done this awful thing alone; she must find some way out, alone. Like touching a festering sore, she put her finger upon that moment when she had shouted her defiance to the sheriff, when she had shouted to feel her strength. She had lost Sug to save others; she had let Johnny-Boy go to save others; and then in a moment of weakness that came from too much strength she had lost all. If she had not shouted to the sheriff, she would have been strong enough to have resisted Booker; she would have been able to tell the comrades herself. Something tightened in her as she remembered and understood the fit of fear she had felt on coming to herself in the dark hallway. A part of her life she thought she had done away with forever had had hold of her then. She had thought the soft, warm past was over; she had thought that it did not mean much when now she sang: "*Hes the Lily of the Valley, the Bright n Mawnin Star*" ... The days when she had sung that song were the days when she had not hoped for anything on this earth, the days when the cold mountain had driven her into the arms of Jesus. She had thought that Sug and Johnny-Boy had taught her to forget Him, to fix her hope upon the fight of black men for freedom. Through the gradual years she had believed and worked with them, had felt strength shed from the grace of their terrible vision. That grace had been upon her when she had let the sheriff slap her down; it had been upon her when she had risen time and again from the floor and faced him. But she had trapped herself with her own hunger; to water the long, dry thirst of her faith; her pride had made a bargain which her flesh could not keep. Her having told the names of Johnny-Boy's comrades was but an incident in a deeper horror. She stood up and looked at the floor while call and counter-call, loyalty and counter-loyalty struggled in her soul. Mired she was between two abandoned worlds, living, but dying without the strength of the grace that either gave. The clearer she felt it the fuller did something well up from the depths of her for release; the more urgent did she feel the need to fling into her black sky another star, another hope, one more terrible vision to give her the strength to live and act. Softly and restlessly she walked about the kitchen, feeling herself naked against the night, the rain, the world; and shamed whenever the thought of Reva's love crossed her mind. She lifted her empty hands and looked at her writhing fingers. Lawd, whut kin Ah do now? She could still wade the creek and get to Foleys Woods before Booker. And then what? How could she manage to see Johnny-Boy or Booker? Again she heard the sheriff's threatening voice: Git yuh a sheet, cause hes gonna be dead! The sheet! Thas it, the *sheet!* Her whole being leaped with will; the long years of her life bent toward a moment of focus, a point. Ah kin go wid mah sheet! Ahll be doin whut he said! Lawd Gawd in Heaven, Ahma go lika nigger woman wid mah windin sheet t git mah dead son! But then what? She stood straight and smiled grimly; she had in her heart the whole meaning of her life; her entire personality was poised on the brink of a total act. Ah know! Ah *know!* She thought of Johnny-Boy's gun in the dresser drawer. Ahll hide the gun in the sheet n go aftah Johnny-Boys body .... She tiptoed to her room, eased out the dresser drawer, and got a sheet. Reva was sleeping; the darkness was filled with her quiet breathing. She groped in the drawer and found the gun. She wound the gun in the sheet and held them both under her apron. Then she stole to the bedside and watched Reva. Lawd, hep her! But mabbe shes bettah off. This had t happen sometime ... She n Johnny-Boy couldna been together in this here South ... N Ah couldnt tell her about Booker. Itll come out awright n she wont nevah know. Reva's trust would never be shaken. She caught her breath as the shucks in the mattress rustled dryly; then all was quiet and she breathed easily again. She tiptoed to the door, down the hall, and stood on the porch. Above her the yellow beacon whirled through the rain. She went over muddy ground, mounted a slope, stopped and looked back at her house. The lamp glowed in her window, and the yellow beacon that swung every few seconds seemed to feed it with light. She turned and started across the fields, holding the gun and sheet tightly, thinking, Po Reva ... Po critter ... Shes fas ersleep...

For the most part she walked with her eyes half shut, her lips tightly compressed, leaning her body against the wind and the driving rain, feeling the pistol in the sheet sagging cold and heavy in her fingers. Already she was getting wet; it seemed that her feet found every puddle of water that stood between the corn rows.

She came to the edge of the creek and paused, wondering at what point was it low. Taking the sheet from under her apron, she wrapped the gun in it so that her finger could be upon the trigger. Ahll cross here, she thought. At first she did not feel the water; her feet were already wet. But the water grew cold as it came up to her knees; she gasped when it reached her waist. Lawd, this creeks high! When she had passed the middle, she knew that she was out of danger. She came out of the water, climbed a grassy hill, walked on, turned a bend and saw the lights of autos gleaming ahead. Yeah; theys still there! She hurried with her head down. Wondah did Ah beat im here? Lawd, Ah *hope* so! A vivid image of Booker's white face hovered a moment before her eyes and a surging will rose up in her so hard and strong that it vanished. She was among the autos now. From nearby came the hoarse voices of the men.

"Hey, yuh!"

She stopped, nervously clutching the sheet. Two white men with shotguns came toward her.

"Whut in hell yuh doin out here?"

She did not answer.

"Didnt yuh hear somebody speak t yuh?"

"Ahm comin aftah mah son," she said humbly.

"Yo *son?*"

"Yessuh."

"What yo son doin out here?"

"The sheriffs got im."

"Holy Scott! Jim, its the niggers ma!"

"Whut yuh got there?" asked one.

"A sheet."

"A *sheet?*"

"Yessuh."

"Fer whut?"

"The sheriff tol me t bring a sheet t git his body."

"Waal, waal..."

"Now, ain tha somethin?"

The white men looked at each other.

"These niggers sho love one ernother," said one.

"N tha ain no lie," said the other.

"Take me t the sheriff," she begged.

"Yuh ain givin us *orders*, is yuh?"

"Nawsuh."

"Well take yuh when wes good n ready."

"Yessuh."

"So yuh wan his body?"

"Yessuh."

"Waal, he ain dead yit."

"They gonna kill im," she said.

"Ef he talks they wont."

"He ain gonna talk," she said.

"How yuh know?"

"Cause he ain."

"We got ways of makin niggers talk."

"Yuh ain got no way fer im."

"Yuh thinka lot of that black Red, don yuh?"

"Hes mah son."

"Why don yuh teach im some sense?"

"Hes mah son," she said again.

"Lissen, ol nigger woman, yuh stand there wid yo hair white. Yuh got bettah sense than t believe tha niggers kin make a revolution…"

"A black republic," said the other one, laughing.

"Take me t the sheriff," she begged.

"Yuh his ma," said one. "Yuh kin make im talk n tell whose in this thing wid im."

"He ain gonna talk," she said.

"Don yuh wan im t live?"

She did not answer.

"C mon, les take her t Bradley."

They grabbed her arms and she clutched hard at the sheet and gun; they led her toward the crowd in the woods. Her feelings were simple; Booker would not tell; she was there with the gun to see to that. The louder became the voices of the men the deeper became her feeling of wanting to right the mistake she had made; of wanting to fight her way back to solid ground. She would stall for time until Booker showed up. Oh, ef theyll only lemme git close t Johnny-Boy! As they led her near the crowd she saw white faces turning and looking at her and heard a rising clamor of voices.

"Whose tha?"

"A nigger woman!"

"Whut she doin out here?"

"This is his ma!" called one of the men.

"Whut she wans?"

"She brought a sheet t cover his body!"

"He ain dead yit!"

"They tryin t make im talk!"

"But he will be dead soon ef he don open up!"

"Say, look! The niggers ma brought a sheet t cover up his body!"

"Now, ain that sweet?"

"Mabbe she wans t hol a prayer meetin!"

"Did she git a preacher?"

"Say, go git Bradley!"

"O.K.!"

The crowd grew quiet. They looked at her curiously; she felt their cold eyes trying to detect some weakness in her. Humbly, she stood with the sheet covering the gun. She had already accepted all that they could do to her.

The sheriff came.

"So yuh brought yuh sheet, hunh?"

"Yessuh," she whispered.

"Looks like them slaps we gave yuh learned yuh some sense, didnt they?"

She did not answer.

"Yuh don need tha sheet. Yo son ain dead yit," he said, reaching toward her.

She backed away, her eyes wide.

"Naw!"

"Now, lissen, Anty!" he said. "There ain no use in yuh ackin a fool! Go in there n tell tha nigger son of yos t tell us whos in this wid im, see? Ah promise we wont kill im ef he talks. We'll let im git outta town."

"There ain nothin Ah kin tell im," she said.

"Yuh wan us t kill im?"

She did not answer. She saw someone lean toward the sheriff and whisper.

"Bring her erlong," the sheriff said.

They led her to a muddy clearing. The rain streamed down through the ghostly glare of the flashlights. As the men formed a semi-circle she saw Johnny-Boy lying in a trough of mud. He was tied with rope; he lay hunched and one side of his face rested in a pool of black water. His eyes were staring questioningly at her.

"Speak t im," said the sheriff.

If she could only tell him why she was here! But that was impossible; she was close to what she wanted and she stared straight before her with compressed lips.

"Say, nigger!" called the sheriff, kicking Johnny-Boy. "Heres yo ma!"

Johnny-Boy did not move or speak. The sheriff faced her again.

"Lissen, Anty," he said. "Yuh got mo say wid im than anybody. Tell im t talk n hava chance. Whut he wanna pertect the other niggers n white folks fer?"

She slid her finger about the trigger of the gun and looked stonily at the mud.

"Go t him," said the sheriff.

She did not move. Her heart was crying out to answer the amazed question in Johnny-Boy's eyes. But there was no way now.

"Waal, yuhre astin fer it. By Gawd, we gotta way to *make* yuh talk t im," he said, turning away. "Say, Tim, git one of them logs n turn that nigger upside-down n put his legs on it!"

A murmur of assent ran through the crowd. She bit her lips; she knew what that meant.

"Yuh wan yo nigger son crippled?" she heard the sheriff ask.

She did not answer. She saw them roll the log up; they lifted Johnny-Boy and laid him on his face and stomach, then they pulled his legs over the log. His kneecaps rested on the sheer top of the log's back and the toes of his shoes pointed groundward. So absorbed was she in watching that she felt that it was she who was being lifted and made ready for torture.

"Git a crowbar!" said the sheriff.

A tall, lank man got a crowbar from a nearby auto and stood over the log. His jaws worked slowly on a wad of tobacco.

"Now, its up t yuh, Anty," the sheriff said. "Tell the man whut t do!"

She looked into the rain. The sheriff turned.

"Mebbe she think wes playin. Ef she don say nothin, then break em at the kneecaps!"

"O.K., Sheriff!"

She stood waiting for Booker. Her legs felt weak; she wondered if she would be able to wait much longer. Over and over she said to herself, Ef he came now Ahd kill em both!

"She ain sayin nothin, Sheriff!"

"Waal, Gawddammit, let im have it!"

The crowbar came down and Johnny-Boy's body lunged in the mud and water. There was a scream. She swayed, holding tight to the gun and sheet.

"Hol im! Git the other leg!"

The crowbar fell again. There was another scream.

"Yuh break em?" asked the sheriff.

The tall man lifted Johnny-Boy's legs and let them drop limply again, dropping rearward from the kneecaps. Johnny-Boy's body lay still. His head had rolled to one side and she could not see his face.

"Jus lika broke sparrow wing," said the man, laughing softly.

Then Johnny-Boy's face turned to her; he screamed.

"Go way, ma! Go way!"

It was the first time she had heard his voice since she had come out to the woods; she all but lost control of herself. She started violently forward, but the sheriff's arm checked her.

"Aw, naw! Yuh had yo chance!" He turned to Johnny-Boy. "She kin go ef yuh talk."

"Mistah, he ain gonna talk," she said.

"Go way, ma!" said Johnny-Boy.

"Shoot im! Don make im suffah so," she begged.

"He'll either talk or he'll never hear yuh ergin," the sheriff said. "Theres other things we kin do t im."

She said nothing.

"Whut yuh come here fer, ma?" Johnny-Boy sobbed.

"Ahm gonna split his eardrums," the sheriff said. "Ef yuh got anythin to say t im yuh bettah say it *now!*"

She closed her eyes. She heard the sheriff's feet sucking in mud. Ah could save im! She opened her eyes; there were shouts of eagerness from the crowd as it pushed in closer.

"Bus em, Sheriff!"

"Fix im so he cant hear!"

"He knows how t do it, too!"

"He busted a Jew boy tha way once!"

She saw the sheriff stoop over Johnny-Boy, place his flat palm over one ear and strike his fist against it with all his might. He placed his palm over the other ear and struck again. Johnny-Boy moaned, his head rolling from side to side, his eyes showing white amazement in a world without sound.

"Yuh wouldnt talk t im when yuh had the chance," said the sheriff. "Try n talk now."

She felt warm tears on her cheeks. She longed to shoot Johnny-Boy and let him go. But if she did that they would take the gun from her, and Booker would tell who the others were. Lawd, hep me! The men were talking loudly now, as though the main business was over. It seemed ages that she stood there watching Johnny-Boy roll and whimper in his world of silence.

"Say, Sheriff, heres somebody lookin fer yuh!"

"Who is it?"

"Ah don know!"

"Bring em in!"

She stiffened and looked around wildly, holding the gun tight. Is tha Booker? Then she held still, feeling that her excitement might betray her. Mabbe Ah kin shoot em both! Mabbe Ah kin shoot *twice!* The sheriff stood in front of her, waiting. The crowd parted and she saw Booker hurrying forward.

"Ah know em all, Sheriff!" he called.

He came full into the muddy clearing where Johnny-Boy lay.

"Yuh mean yuh got the names?"

"Sho! The ol nigger..."

She saw his lips hang open and silent when he saw her. She stepped forward and raised the sheet.

"Whut..."

She fired, once; then, without pausing, she turned, hearing them yell. She aimed at Johnny-Boy, but they had their arms around her, bearing her to the ground, clawing at the sheet in her hand. She glimpsed Booker lying sprawled in the mud, on his face, his hands stretched out before him; then a cluster of yelling men blotted him out. She lay without struggling, looking upward through the rain at the white faces above her. And she was suddenly at peace; they were not a white mountain now; they were not pushing her any longer to the edge of life. Its awright…

"She shot Booker!"

"She hada gun in the sheet!"

"She shot im right thu the head!"

"Whut she shoot im fer?"

"Kill the bitch!"

"Ah *thought* somethin wuz wrong bout her!"

"Ah wuz fer givin it t her from the firs!"

"Thas whut yuh git fer treatin a nigger nice!"

"Say, Bookers dead!"

She stopped looking into the white faces, stopped listening. She waited, giving up her life before they took it from her; she had done what she wanted. Ef only Johnny-Boy … She looked at him; he lay looking at her with tired eyes. Ef she could only tell im! But he lay already buried in a grave of silence.

"Whut yuh kill im fer, hunh?"

It was the sheriff's voice; she did not answer.

"Mabbe she wuz shootin at yuh, Sheriff?"

"Whut yuh kill im fer?"

She felt the sheriff's foot come into her side; she closed her eyes.

"Yuh black bitch!"

"Let her have it!"

"Yuh reckon she foun out bout Booker?"

"She mighta."

"Jesus Chris, whut yuh dummies *waitin* on!"

"Yeah; kill her!"

"Kill em *both!*"

"Let her know her nigger sons dead firs!"

She turned her head toward Johnny-Boy; he lay looking puzzled in a world beyond the reach of voices. At leas he cant hear, she thought.

"C mon, let im have it!"

She listened to hear what Johnny-Boy could not. They came, two of them, one right behind the other; so close together that they sounded like one shot. She did not look at Johnny-Boy now; she looked at the white faces of the men, hard and wet in the glare of the flashlights.

"Yuh hear tha, nigger woman?"

"Did tha surprise im? Hes in hell now wonderin whut hit im!"

"C mon! Give it t her, Sheriff!"

"Lemme shoot her, Sheriff! It wuz mah pal she shot!"

"Awright, Pete! Thas fair ernuff!"

She gave up as much of her life as she could before they took it from her. But the sound of the shot and the streak of fire that tore its way through her chest forced her to live again, intensely. She had not moved, save for the slight jarring impact of the bullet. She felt the heat of her own blood warming her cold, wet back. She yearned suddenly to talk. "Yuh didn't git whut yuh wanted! N yuh ain gonna nevah git it! Yuh didn't kill me; Ah come here by mahsef…" She felt rain falling into her wide-open, dimming eyes and heard faint voices. Her lips moved soundlessly. *Yuh didn't git yuh didnt yuh didnt* … Focused and pointed she was, buried in the depths of her star, swallowed in its peace and strength; and not feeling her flesh growing cold, cold as the rain that fell from the invisible sky upon the doomed living and the dead that never dies.

—1938, 1940

Credits

This page constitutes an extension of the copyright page. We have made every effort to trace the ownership of all copyrighted material and to secure permission from copyright holders. In the event of any question arising as to the use of any material, we will be pleased to make the necessary corrections in future printings. Thanks are due to the following authors, publishers, and agents for permission to use the material indicated.

Boyle, Kay

"A Communication to Nancy Cunnard" in *Collected Poems/Kay Boyle.* Alfred A. Knopf, 1962. Copyright © 1962 by Kay Boyle. All rights reserved.

Brown, Sterling A.

"Bitter Fruit of the Tree" from *The Collected Poems of Sterling A. Brown*, edited by Michael S. Harper. Copyright © 1980 by Sterling A. Brown. Reprinted by permission of HarperCollins Publishers.

"Remembering Nat Turner" from *The Collected Poems of Sterling A. Brown*, edited by Michael S. Harper. Copyright © 1980 by Sterling A. Brown. Reprinted by permission of HarperCollins Publishers.

"Song of Triumph" from *The Collected Poems of Sterling A. Brown*, edited by Michael S. Harper. Copyright © 1980 by Sterling A. Brown. Reprinted by permission of HarperCollins Publishers.

"Strong Men" from *The Collected Poems of Sterling A. Brown*, edited by Michael S. Harper. Copyright 1932 Harcourt Brace & Cop.; renewed © 1960 by Sterling A. Brown. Originally appeared in *Southern Road.* Reprinted by permission of HarperCollins Publishers.

Bonner, Marita

"On Being Young—A Woman—and Colored" from *Frye Street & Environs: The Collected Works of Marita Bonner* edited by Joyce Flynn. Beacon Press, 1987. © 1987 by Joyce Flynn and Joyce Occomy Stricklin. Reprinted by permission of Beacon Press, Boston.

Hughes, Langston

"Harlem (2)" from *Collected Poems of Langston Hughes,* edited by Arnold Rampersad with David Roessel, Associate Editor, copyright © 1951 by Langston Hughes. Used by permission of Alfred A. Knopf, a division of Random House, Inc.

"Mulatto" from *Collected Poems of Langston Hughes*, edited by Arnold Rampersad with David Roessel, Associate Editor, copyright © 1994 by The Estate of Langston Hughes. Used by permission of Alfred A. Knopf, a division of Random House, Inc.

"Song for a Dark Girl" from *Collected Poems of Langston Hughes*, edited by Arnold Rampersad with David Roessel, Associate Editor, copyright © 1994 by The Estate of Langston Hughes. Used by permission of Alfred A. Knopf, a division of Random House, Inc.

Hurston, Zora Neale

"How it Feels to be Colored Me" in *I Love Myself When I am Laughing...And Then Again When I am Looking Mean and Impressive....* Edited by Alice Walker. Feminist Press, 1979.

Toomer, Jean

"Blood-Burning Moon" from *Cane*. Copyright © 1923 by Boni & Liveright, renewed 1951 by Jean Toomer. Used by permission of Liveright Publishing Corporation.

"Portrait in Georgia" from *Cane*. Copyright © 1923 by Boni & Liveright, renewed 1951 by Jean Toomer. Used by permission of Liveright Publishing Corporation.

White, Walter

"I Investigate Lynching" in *The American Mercury*, vol. 16, 1929, pp. 74-88. Copyright © by Walter White.

Wright, Richard

"Bright and Morning Star" from *Uncle Tom's Children*. Copyright © 1936, 1937, 1938 by Richard Wright. Copyright renewed © 1964, 1965, 1966 by Ellen Wright. Reprinted by permission of HarperCollins Publishers.

"The Ethics of Living Jim Crow" from *Uncle Tom's Children*. Copyright © 1936, 1937, 1938 by Richard Wright. Copyright renewed © 1964, 1965, 1966 by Ellen Wright. Reprinted by permission of HarperCollins Publishers.